THE Grief Adjustment Guide

A PATHWAY THROUGH PAIN

D1551846

*Charlotte
Greeson*

*Mary
Hollingsworth*

*Michael P.
Washburn*

QUESTAR
Publishers, Inc.

"I recently lost my father, and my mother has been diagnosed with a severe illness. Grief is always with us. The authors of *The Grief Adjustment Guide* have done an admirable job combining the difficult necessities of personal and legal documentation with the important, yet often neglected, dynamics of grief work. This book sets out the topics which must be faced in a logical, systematic, yet caring manner."

ROBERT W. BURNS
author of *Through the Whirlwind*

"Any time life turns left — as it does when someone dies — we need to find a safe and sane place from which to navigate our journey. *The Grief Adjustment Guide* is such a place. It is practical, thorough, detailed, sensitive and hopeful. Someone you know could use this book."

TERRY HERSHEY
counseling director, Vashon, Washington

"What a joy to have available on the grief journey a new and practically helpful publication that can be useful to the helper as well as the helpee. Charlotte Greeson, Mary Hollingsworth and Mike Washburn are to be congratulated for giving us a new tool!"

MARY RANDOLPH
Director of Single Adult Ministries
Asbury United Methodist Church, Tulsa, Oklahoma

THE GRIEF ADJUSTMENT GUIDE

© 1990 by Charlotte Greeson, Mary Hollingsworth and Michael P. Washburn
Administered by Creative Enterprises, 3950 Fossil Creek Boulevard, Suite 203, Fort Worth, Texas 76137

Published by
QUESTAR PUBLISHERS, INC.
Sisters, Oregon

Printed in the United States of America

International Standard Book Number: 0-945564-37-6

THE GRIEF ADJUSTMENT GUIDE offers practical help…

to those who have just lost a loved one through death —
whether it happened only hours ago, or at some
other point in the past few months;

AND

to those facing the imminent death of a loved one,
and who wish to plan ahead of time — sensibly and
sensitively — in order to lessen the burden of details
and decision-making when their loved one departs.

• **If your loved one's death has just occurred,** and you are faced
suddenly with pressing decisions concerning the funeral, burial,
and other matters— ***look at Sections 1 and 2 to find immediate help*** as you proceed through these difficult moments and
hours. The rest of the book will offer very valuable help, too,
and quite soon — but for today, it can wait.

• **If your loved one's death occurred anywhere from several
days to several weeks ago,** you have already made it through
the funeral and the first days of shock and sorrow. But you no
doubt are feeling the anguish of grief as much as ever, combined with the burden of still having many decisions to make
and details to take care of. ***Begin with Sections 3 and 4 to find
the best help at this stage in the grief process,*** and plan to continue on through the rest of the book.

• **If your loved one has not yet passed away,** but you've wisely
chosen to begin planning for the inevitable, ***Sections 1 and 2***
will offer a helpful, dependable plan and format for sound and
sensitive decisionmaking. You'll also gain much by looking over
the rest of the book as well. *You will always be grateful* for having
done this thinking and planning at this time.

Special thanks

WE WANT to sincerely thank the following people whose contributions and encouragement made this project possible.

Sher Abernathy, MSW, CSW
Medical Social Worker, Dialysis Associates
Fort Worth, Texas

Linda Dabney

Teri Duke

Duffy Lewis
and the
Grief Adjustment Team
Richland Hills Church of Christ
Fort Worth, Texas

William G. "Bill" Southern, LUTCF
Connecticut Mutual Life Insurance Company
Fort Worth, Texas

Sharon Washburn

and, of course,
Don Jacobson and
Questar Publishers

this book belongs to:

_____

_____

_____

*Love is stronger than death. So, I
must be content to know that love is not
affected by death—it doesn't end, it doesn't
diminish, it doesn't change.*

*Instead, love is immortalized and eternalized
through death. And the possibility of that love ever
being damaged or broken is eliminated
forever.*

I'll put my trust in love.

MARY HOLLINGSWORTH
RAINBOWS

Contents

Contents

Contents

A Personal Word
from the Authors

YOU ARE NOT ALONE, though you probably *feel* very alone right now. Practically every person who has ever lived, including your friends, family members and neighbors, has suffered or will suffer the kind of grief you are now facing. Grief is inevitable. It's part of the natural life-and-death cycle. As one griever put it, "Of all the people you will know in your lifetime, *you* are the only one you will never leave nor lose."

All three of us who are writing this guide have lost mates, parents and grandparents to death. We understand your grief. And yet we have survived...and you will, too, though your heart is now broken and heavy. In spite of our great losses, life goes on — and so must we.

YOU MAY BE overwhelmed by grief right now. You may be thinking, *I'll never adjust to this grief...NEVER! I just don't think I can go on.*

This book will not take your grief away. Nothing can do that. You will always remember with longing the one you have cared for and lost. The question is, what will you *do* with your grief? Will you allow grief to rule your life and drive you to total despair, or will you work patiently to adjust to your grief and get on with your life?

The Grief Adjustment Guide is practical and easy to use during the difficult days and nights of grief. It gives you plenty of space to record important information and to keep track of the innumerable details that must be handled. It also gives you a place to record happy memories, feelings of loss, the down times and times of growth. It will be a friend to you in your time of need.

This guide will give you professional advice and practical pointers on how to adjust to your new life in which grief currently plays a major part. As you continue using this book, in time you will find grief beginning to play a lesser role in your life.

ONE WORD OF CAUTION: This guide cannot take the place of the professional resource people you will need to direct various complicated aspects of grief adjustment, including certain legal, financial, and emotional matters. This book is a memory jogger and workbook

"...out of your loss is an interconnectedness with all humanity— for you are one with everyone who has ever mourned."

—RUSTY BERKUS
TO HEAL AGAIN

helping you know when and where to call on the professional resources you will need. It serves also as a place to record answers to important questions and concerns.

How this guide is organized

GRIEF BEGINS, unfortunately, in the midst of the turmoil of putting to rest the one you have lost. Hundreds of decisions must be made during the first few days of your grief. Because of that, this guide begins by showing you how to make funeral arrangements and how to perform the follow-up tasks, even while your grief is growing from initial shock into aching reality. Handling these final arrangements for your lost one is the first practical step you will take in adjusting to your grief.

When these bittersweet tasks have been completed, you will be ready to tackle the difficult chore of dealing with your grief. Section 5 in this book (entitled "A Time to Refocus: Beginning Again") will help you identify where you are in the grief process and help you determine how to begin working patiently on the issues of grief that face you. We especially recommend your regular use of the Journal pages (also found in Section 5) to record your progressive feelings and accomplishments.

Once you've found where you are in the grief process, this guide will assist you in getting organized and in planning for the future. Legal, financial, emotional and other matters are discussed here, and recommendations are made that have been followed successfully by thousands of people experiencing loss.

THE PURPOSE of this guide is to help you and others like you to work through grief and to adjust to a new and different life, a life more mature because it has been touched by grief. It is our hope that this guide can, in some small, practical way, help you gently along the pathway of grief adjustment to find peace, contentment and personal challenge in your new life.

CHARLOTTE GREESON
MARY HOLLINGSWORTH
MIKE WASHBURN

IMMEDIATE CONCERNS

1

Your First Plans

WHILE WE DO NOT *choose* death, it *is* an inevitable door through which each person must walk. When loved ones approach and enter this doorway into the next life, it becomes our privilege to plan a suitable farewell for them from this life.

This first section of THE GRIEF ADJUSTMENT GUIDE is intended to make those arrangements as uncomplicated for you as possible.

SELECTING THE FUNERAL FACILITY that's right for you and your family is almost always done by considering reputation or availability. The skill and kindness with which a particular funeral director and facility serve families is readily known in most communities. If you have had no previous experience with a funeral director or facility in your area, ask a trusted, experienced relative or friend for his or her recommendation.

You can also verify a facility's reputation by calling the Better Business Bureau in your area, or asking the minister of your church.

When you have made an initial selection, don't be afraid to ask questions of the funeral home staff. They are there to serve you and will be glad to answer questions you have or to assist in any possible way with your plans.

The best time to think about a funeral is when you don't have to. In other words, it's best to select a funeral facility when you are not under the emotional strain of having lost someone near to you. Visit the funeral home and examine its facilities. Ask about prices and services offered. Simply put: If possible, plan ahead.

How do I choose a funeral facility?

What should I expect from a funeral home?

DEALING WITH a funeral facility can be a tense time, largely because most people are not prepared. Decisions must be made during intense emotional crisis. Also, the process is unfamiliar and there is precious little time to think things through.

These anxieties should not stand in the way of getting the service you wish because funeral homes are established to serve people in the midst of their grief.

You should expect the funeral home to make available to you an itemized list showing the costs of services and products offered (most states require funeral homes to publish such a list). Included should be prices for the following:

- transferring the deceased to the funeral home from the hospital or other place of death
- embalming
- use of funeral facility for family and friends to view the remains
- use of the facility for the funeral service or ceremonies
- transferring the remains to the burial site, via a church (if desired)
- use of funeral home's cars (hearses, limousines)
- itemized services for the funeral home's staff
- caskets or other containers
- burial clothes, if needed
- burial vault or other outer enclosures, where applicable
- graveside expenses, such as ground preparation, use of funeral facility's awning and chairs for graveside services, etc.
- flowers

When your choices are complete and the funeral director is fully informed of your wishes, ask for a written contract to be prepared immediately showing *all* expenses to be incurred. Don't wait until the services have been performed to finalize the contract and your expenses.

CHOOSING A CEMETERY or alternative resting place is an important and highly personal matter. The funeral home may assist in your selection, but the ultimate choice must be that of the family or friends. As our society becomes more mobile, this choice becomes more difficult for some people. Here are some questions to answer before making your final choice:

1. Has a burial plot or other interment location already been purchased for the deceased? *yes___ no___*
   If so, where? _____
2. Is this facility within my practical price range? *yes___ no___*
   cost: $_____
3. Is the location desirable? *yes___ no___*
   comments: _____
4. Is it accessible to family? *yes___ no___*
   comments: _____
5. What about the deceased's family roots and heritage? For instance, is there a family plot or cemetery that would be preferable? *yes___ no___* If so, where is it located?
   _____
6. Does this cemetery provide continual care for the grounds and graves? *yes___ no___ cost:* $_____
   describe: _____
7. Does the cemetery provide flowers for the graves at significant times of the year (such as Christmas, Easter, Mother's Day, Father's Day)? *yes___ no___ cost:* $_____
   describe services: _____
8. What types of headstones or grave markers are allowed in this cemetery? _____
   Will you be satisfied for years to come with that type of memorial stone? *yes___ no___ comments:* _____
9. Does this facility allow above-ground burial vaults?
   yes___ no___ If so, what are its requirements? _____
   _____
10. What is the cost for below-ground vaults? $_____ And what are the requirements? _____
11. Is this cemetery safe from flooding? *yes___ no___*
    comments: _____

How do I choose a monument?

MANY FUNERAL FACILITIES will be able to assist you in choosing a proper headstone or monument to mark the interment place of the deceased. Otherwise, ask a friend or relative (someone with previous experience in selecting a headstone) for the name of a reputable, local monument company. If that does not supply an answer, check your telephone book's *Yellow Pages*.

As you select a memorial stone, keep in mind that it's intended to last for decades, possibly even centuries. A marker records the deceased's life history for descendants and friends. The marker should be a reflection of the deceased's personality and wishes, if possible. Durability, style, and the words to be engraved on the marker are the three most important considerations, other than cost.

Answers to the following questions are important when selecting a monument.

1. Has a monument already been selected? *yes___ no___* Is it already in place at the interment site? *yes___ no___*
2. Keeping in mind the requirements and restrictions set by the interment facility you have chosen, what size monument do you want for the deceased? *large___ average___ small___*
3. Planning ahead, do you need to purchase a single or a double monument? *single___ double___*
4. (The monument company will likely have a selection of stones from which to choose, and perhaps a catalog from which to select an appropriate marker. Look around; do not make this decision in haste.)
   name/description of marker selected: _____
   color of stone: _____
   material marker is made of: _____
5. Is the stone you have selected within your practical price range? *yes___ no___ cost: $_____*
6. If you selected a *single* marker, how should the marker be engraved?

   _____
   _____
   _____
   _____
   _____

7. If you selected a *double* marker, how should the marker be engraved? (Often the name and date of birth of the surviving

person are also engraved on the marker at the same time as the deceased's, leaving only the date of death to be engraved later.)

_____

_____

_____

_____

_____

_____

8. Will the monument company engrave and install the monument? *yes___ no___* If so, what are the extra costs? $_____

9. How quickly will the monument company be able to secure the proper stone, have it engraved and installed at the interment site? _____

10. Name of monument company: _____

   contact person: _____

   address: _____

   city/state/zip: _____

   telephone number: _____

11. Date monument was purchased: _____

12. How monument was paid for:

   ___ cash (Did you get a receipt?)

   ___ check (Your check number: _____)

   ___ American Express

   ___ VISA

   ___ MasterCard

   ___ other: _____

Requiem

Under the wide and starry sky
Dig the grave and let me lie.
Glad did I live and gladly die,
And I laid me down with a will.

This be the verse you grave for me:
Here he lies where he longed to be;
Home is the sailor, home from the sea,
And the hunter home from the hill.

ROBERT LEWIS STEVENSON

Alternatives to burial

SOME PEOPLE prefer alternatives to ground burial. Here are some available alternatives you and your loved ones may wish to consider:

CREMATION — If cremation is chosen, the crematory selected may require some type of container for the deceased. This container may be in the form of a sturdy cardboard container, a wooden box or a standard casket of your choice. All these arrangements can be coordinated for you by the funeral facility you select.

You may choose to dispose of the deceased's remains in a number of ways, according to various state laws and municipal regulations:
- privately scattered. *Where?* _____
- scattered at sea. *Where?* _____
- interred in a cemetery. *Where?* _____
- kept by the family. *Where?* _____
- other: _____

DONATION TO SCIENCE OR MEDICAL FACILITY — An anatomical gift to a medical school or scientific research facility is another alternative to ground burial. These arrangements can be made directly through the medical school or through the funeral home. This can be done in advance, when appropriate, to avoid complications at the time of death.

If this alternative is selected, a portion of the cost of preparation and embalming is often assumed by the receiving medical or scientific facility and will be paid by the Anatomical Board. In some instances, the donor or donor's family may be required to pay the cost of transporting the deceased to the receiving facility.

science or medical facility chosen: _____
contact person: _____
address: _____
city/state/zip: _____
telephone number: _____

ORGAN DONATION TO SCIENCE OR MEDICINE — A person may choose to donate one or all organs of the body but not the body itself. This may be accomplished by signing the proper documents, which are available at hospitals and funeral homes. Once signed, such documents should be filed safely in a location known to next of kin or those who will be attending to the donor's last wishes.

location of donor authorization documents: _____

IMMEDIATE DISPOSAL — "Immediate disposal" usually designates disposal of the deceased's remains with no attending rites, ceremonies, or services. This choice usually includes transfer of the remains, sanitary care in compliance with state and local laws, preparation of and filing of the necessary authorizations and consents, completion of the death certificate and burial transit permit, and provision of a container for handling the remains. Your local funeral director can advise you about the details of this alternative to ground burial.

Documents detailing the arrangements for immediate disposal should be filed in a safe place known to the next of kin or person who will carry out the deceased's last wishes.

location of immediate disposal documents: _____

Don't Send Me Roses

Don't send me roses when I go;
I can't see them, I can't know;
I cannot feel their petalled pleats
Or smell their mortal sweets.

Don't mourn when my soul starts to roam;
I'll only just have journeyed home;
I'm not so very far away—
Just a heartbeat some sweet day.

Don't think of me as lost forever;
I'll wait for you by life's pure river;
My spirit lives within your heart;
My love for you will ne'er depart.

Don't stand at my grave and weep;
I'm not shrouded in morbid sleep;
Look up to God's immortal sky;
I'm safe with Him; I did not die.

MARY HOLLINGSWORTH

Special selections

IF A TRADITIONAL funeral service and ground burial has been chosen, it is necessary to select such items as a casket and burial clothing and jewelry. If possible, personal preplanning is the best way to ensure that last wishes are accurately understood; otherwise, next of kin or friends will need to make the selections.

(In Section 2 you'll find help for making special music selections and deciding other aspects of the funeral and interment services.)

CASKET OR ALTERNATIVE —
type of construction (e.g., wood, metal): _____

color choice: _____ price: $ _____

guarantees/warranties: _____

other considerations: _____

BURIAL CLOTHING —

man's clothing
suit: _____ tie: _____

shirt: _____ shoes: _____

belt and buckle:_____ suspenders: _____

underclothes: _____ glasses: _____

other: _____

woman's clothing
dress: _____ skirt and blouse: _____

belt: _____ shoes: _____

hair clip(s): _____ scarf: _____

underclothes: _____ glasses: _____

other: _____

military attire
uniform: _____ hat/cap: _____

scarf: _____ belt and buckle: _____

shoes: _____ underclothes: _____

other: _____

JEWELRY — There is often disagreement about the advisability of leaving jewelry on the deceased. A common practice is to display the jewelry on the body during the funeral service itself, and then simply remove it prior to burial. (If this practice is chosen, make certain the funeral director is informed in order to remove the jewelry at the proper time.) By law in most areas, a body that has been interred may not be later exhumed to retrieve jewelry.

man's jewelry

ring(s): _____ pin(s):_____

watch: _____ tie tack: _____

belt buckle: _____ bracelet: _____

necklace: _____

woman's jewelry

ring(s): _____ pin(s): _____

watch: _____ bracelet(s): _____

necklace: _____ anklet: _____

earrings: _____ hairpins or clips: _____

military jewelry

ring(s): _____ pin(s):_____

watch: _____ tie tack: _____

belt buckle: _____ bracelet: _____

military ribbons/bars/stripes: _____

_____

A TIME TO WEEP

2

Planning the Funeral Service

AS YOU PLAN A SUITABLE FAREWELL for your loved one, use this section to guide your many decisions — and to give you a place to record the information for reference and safekeeping.

facility chosen: _____

contact person: _____

address: _____

city/state/zip: _____

telephone number: _____

notes: _____

_____

_____

_____

Funeral facility

AT THIS DIFFICULT TIME it may be helpful to ask others to share the load of notifying family and friends of their loss. Perhaps one good way to facilitate this task is to ask one or two family members to call the other family members, and ask one or two friends to call other friends, neighbors, and co-workers.

It is helpful to have funeral details finalized (particularly the date, time, and place of the service) prior to making these calls, to eliminate the expense and time required to make further contact.

Notifying family, friends, and others

Family members to notify

name: _____
address: _____
city/state/zip: _____
telephone number: _____
relationship to deceased: _____

name: _____
address: _____
city/state/zip: _____
telephone number: _____
relationship to deceased: _____

name: _____
address: _____
city/state/zip: _____
telephone number: _____
relationship to deceased: _____

name: _____
address: _____
city/state/zip: _____
telephone number: _____
relationship to deceased: _____

name: _____
address: _____
city/state/zip: _____
telephone number: _____
relationship to deceased: _____

name: _____
address: _____
city/state/zip: _____
telephone number: _____
relationship to deceased: _____

name: _____
address: _____
city/state/zip: _____
telephone number: _____
relationship to deceased: _____

name: _____

address: _____
city/state/zip: _____
telephone number: _____
relationship to deceased: _____

name: _____
address: _____
city/state/zip: _____
telephone number: _____
relationship to deceased: _____

name: _____
address: _____
city/state/zip: _____
telephone number: _____
relationship to deceased: _____

name: _____
address: _____
city/state/zip: _____
telephone number: _____
relationship to deceased: _____

name: _____
address: _____
city/state/zip: _____
telephone number: _____
relationship to deceased: _____

name: _____
address: _____
city/state/zip: _____
telephone number: _____
relationship to deceased: _____

name: _____
address: _____
city/state/zip: _____
telephone number: _____
relationship to deceased: _____

name: _____
address: _____
city/state/zip: _____
telephone number: _____
relationship to deceased: _____

name: _____
address: _____
city/state/zip: _____
telephone number: _____
relationship to deceased: _____

name: _____
address: _____
city/state/zip: _____
telephone number: _____
relationship to deceased: _____

name: _____
address: _____
city/state/zip: _____
telephone number: _____
relationship to deceased: _____

name: _____
address: _____
city/state/zip: _____
telephone number: _____
relationship to deceased: _____

name: _____
address: _____
city/state/zip: _____
telephone number: _____
relationship to deceased: _____

name: _____
address: _____
city/state/zip: _____
telephone number: _____
relationship to deceased: _____

Friends to notify

name: _____
address: _____
city/state/zip: _____
telephone number: _____
interests, etc., shared with deceased: _____

name: _____
address: _____
city/state/zip: _____
telephone number: _____
interests, etc., shared with deceased: _____

name: _____
address: _____
city/state/zip: _____
telephone number: _____
interests, etc., shared with deceased: _____

name: _____
address: _____
city/state/zip: _____
telephone number: _____
interests, etc., shared with deceased: _____

name: _____
address: _____
city/state/zip: _____
telephone number: _____
interests, etc., shared with deceased: _____

name: _____
address: _____
city/state/zip: _____
telephone number: _____
interests, etc., shared with deceased: _____

name: _____
address: _____
city/state/zip: _____
telephone number: _____
interests, etc., shared with deceased: _____

**Friends
to notify**

(continued)

name: _____

address: _____

city/state/zip: _____

telephone number: _____

interests, etc., shared with deceased: _____

name: _____

address: _____

city/state/zip: _____

telephone number: _____

interests, etc., shared with deceased: _____

name: _____

address: _____

city/state/zip: _____

telephone number: _____

interests, etc., shared with deceased: _____

name: _____

address: _____

city/state/zip: _____

telephone number: _____

interests, etc., shared with deceased: _____

name: _____

address: _____

city/state/zip: _____

telephone number: _____

interests, etc., shared with deceased: _____

name: _____

address: _____

city/state/zip: _____

telephone number: _____

interests, etc., shared with deceased: _____

name: _____

address: _____

city/state/zip: _____

telephone number: _____

interests, etc., shared with deceased: _____

name: _____
address: _____
city/state/zip: _____
telephone number: _____
interests, etc., shared with deceased: _____

name: _____
address: _____
city/state/zip: _____
telephone number: _____
interests, etc., shared with deceased: _____

name: _____
address: _____
city/state/zip: _____
telephone number: _____
interests, etc., shared with deceased: _____

name: _____
address: _____
city/state/zip: _____
telephone number: _____
interests, etc., shared with deceased: _____

name: _____
address: _____
city/state/zip: _____
telephone number: _____
interests, etc., shared with deceased: _____

name: _____
address: _____
city/state/zip: _____
telephone number: _____
interests, etc., shared with deceased: _____

name: _____
address: _____
city/state/zip: _____
telephone number: _____
interests, etc., shared with deceased: _____

Friends to notify
(continued)

name: _____
address: _____
city/state/zip: _____
telephone number: _____
interests, etc., shared with deceased: _____

name: _____
address: _____
city/state/zip: _____
telephone number: _____
interests, etc., shared with deceased: _____

name: _____
address: _____
city/state/zip: _____
telephone number: _____
interests, etc., shared with deceased: _____

name: _____
address: _____
city/state/zip: _____
telephone number: _____
interests, etc., shared with deceased: _____

name: _____
address: _____
city/state/zip: _____
telephone number: _____
interests, etc., shared with deceased: _____

name: _____
address: _____
city/state/zip: _____
telephone number: _____
interests, etc., shared with deceased: _____

name: _____
address: _____
city/state/zip: _____
telephone number: _____
interests, etc., shared with deceased: _____

name: _____
address: _____
city/state/zip: _____
telephone number: _____
interests, etc., shared with deceased: _____

name: _____
address: _____
city/state/zip: _____
telephone number: _____
interests, etc., shared with deceased: _____

name: _____
address: _____
city/state/zip: _____
telephone number: _____
interests, etc., shared with deceased: _____

name: _____
address: _____
city/state/zip: _____
telephone number: _____
interests, etc., shared with deceased: _____

name: _____
address: _____
city/state/zip: _____
telephone number: _____
interests, etc., shared with deceased: _____

name: _____
address: _____
city/state/zip: _____
telephone number: _____
interests, etc., shared with deceased: _____

name: _____
address: _____
city/state/zip: _____
telephone number: _____
interests, etc., shared with deceased: _____

Business or professional associates to notify

name: _____
company: _____
address: _____
city/state/zip: _____
telephone number: _____

name: _____
company: _____
address: _____
city/state/zip: _____
telephone number: _____

name: _____
company: _____
address: _____
city/state/zip: _____
telephone number: _____

name: _____
company: _____
address: _____
city/state/zip: _____
telephone number: _____

name: _____
company: _____
address: _____
city/state/zip: _____
telephone number: _____

name: _____
company: _____
address: _____
city/state/zip: _____
telephone number: _____

name: _____
company: _____
address: _____
city/state/zip: _____
telephone number: _____

name: _____

company: _____

address: _____

city/state/zip: _____

telephone number: _____

name: _____

company: _____

address: _____

city/state/zip: _____

telephone number: _____

name: _____

company: _____

address: _____

city/state/zip: _____

telephone number: _____

name: _____

company: _____

address: _____

city/state/zip: _____

telephone number: _____

name: _____

company: _____

address: _____

city/state/zip: _____

telephone number: _____

name: _____

company: _____

address: _____

city/state/zip: _____

telephone number: _____

name: _____

company: _____

address: _____

city/state/zip: _____

telephone number: _____

Organiza-tions to notify

IN ADDITION to business associates, other organizations and groups with whom the deceased was associated will likely need to be notified of their loss — such as church, service organizations, professional associations, social clubs or groups, civic groups, committees, veterans groups, and so on.

Depending on the relationship of the deceased to each of these organizations, it may be more appropriate and realistic to notify them by mail, after the memorial services have been held, than by phone. Other family members and close friends can help you determine the urgency of notifying these groups in advance.

organization: _____

contact person: _____

address: _____

city/state/zip: _____

telephone number: _____

association with deceased: _____

organization: _____

contact person: _____

address: _____

city/state/zip: _____

telephone number: _____

association with deceased: _____

organization: _____

contact person: _____

address: _____

city/state/zip: _____

telephone number: _____

association with deceased: _____

organization: _____

contact person: _____

address: _____

city/state/zip: _____

telephone number: _____

association with deceased: _____

organization: _____

contact person: _____

address: _____

city/state/zip: _____

telephone number: _____

association with deceased: _____

organization: _____

contact person: _____

address: _____

city/state/zip: _____

telephone number: _____

association with deceased: _____

organization: _____

contact person: _____

address: _____

city/state/zip: _____

telephone number: _____

association with deceased: _____

organization: _____

contact person: _____

address: _____

city/state/zip: _____

telephone number: _____

association with deceased: _____

organization: _____

contact person: _____

address: _____

city/state/zip: _____

telephone number: _____

association with deceased: _____

organization: _____

contact person: _____

address: _____

city/state/zip: _____

telephone number: _____

association with deceased: _____

Organizations
to notify

(continued)

Planning the obituary

YOUR LOCAL NEWSPAPER will typically provide a form asking pertinent questions about the deceased and his or her family to properly structure the obituary. Below is an example of that form. It is included here for your convenience (and for preplanning, if possible).

deceased's legal name: _____

nickname of deceased, if commonly used: _____

date of death: month/day/year: _____

city and state of residence: _____

age at death: _____ place of death: _____

MEMORIAL SERVICE:

day of week/date/time: _____

place: _____

place of interment or alternative: _____

deceased's place of birth: _____

if foreign born, how long in this country? _____

deceased's usual occupation: _____

industry or business: _____

retired? *yes___ no___*

if active, current position: _____

deceased's military service record: *from _____to _____*

rank achieved: _____

military decorations or honors: _____

_____

deceased's memberships:

_____
_____
_____
_____
_____

deceased's notable accomplishments:

_____
_____
_____
_____
_____
_____

deceased's marital status: _____

spouse's full name: _____

if spouse is not surviving, year of spouse's death:_____

other surviving family:`(indicate name and city of residence)

sons:

_____

_____

_____

_____

daughters:

_____

_____

_____

_____

mother: _____

father: _____

brothers:

_____

_____

_____

_____

sisters:

_____

_____

_____

_____

grandparents:

_____

_____

_____

_____

number of: *grandchildren:* _____ *great-grandchildren:* _____
        great-great-grandchildren: _____

other survivors of note:

_____

_____

_____

_____

Planning the memorial service

THE INFORMATION on this page will be required for many purposes during the months following a loss. It is best that the information be recorded *in ink* immediately upon determination, for accuracy and permanence.

place: _____

day of week/date/time: _____

person(s) presiding: _____

  title, or relationship to deceased: _____

person presenting obituary: _____

  title, or relationship to deceased: _____

pall bearers: (indicate name and relationship to deceased)

_____

_____

_____

_____

_____

_____

_____

_____

musicians: (indicate name and relationship to deceased)

_____

_____

_____

_____

other participants: (indicate name, and form of participation)

_____

_____

_____

_____

deceased's special wishes: _____

_____

_____

_____

_____

AN INDIVIDUAL'S TASTE in music is highly personal and subjective. To properly represent someone's musical wishes, it is best if that person has preplanned his or her own music selections. If that was not possible, the selection of music becomes the responsibility of the next of kin or friends.

List special music choices here (indicate *song title, author/arranger,* and *publisher*):

_____
_____
_____
_____
_____
_____

type of performance preferred:
soloist:___ quartet:___ octet:___ other ensemble:___ full choir:___

accompaniment: *piano :___ organ :___ a cappella:___*
other :_____

Music

THE ORDER of a memorial service is strictly a matter of personal choice. There are no hard-and-fast rules to follow. Cultural traditions are often followed, but personal preference should be the ultimate guide. The service should be organized and carried out in a way that fits the personality of the deceased, and that is appropriate for the family members and friends in attendance.

Special elements are sometimes included to make the memorial service more personal and memorable (see the end of this section for suggestions).

On the next page is the outline of a typical, traditional memorial service held in a church or funeral facility. Often this order of service is printed and handed out to those attending the service to help them participate in a meaningful and orderly way.

Planning the order of service

TRADITIONAL ORDER OF SERVICE

Richland Hills Family Singers .... *"How Great Thou Art"*

Johnson & Smith Funeral Home .... *Seating of the Family*

Tina Walton .... *"Precious Memories"*

Jon Jones .... *Eulogy*

Richland Hills Family Singers .... *"Peace, Perfect Peace"*

Don Phillips .... *Remarks to the Family*

Prayer

Richland Hills Family Singers .... *"Till We Meet Again"*

Congregation .... *Viewing*

Exit of Family

Order of service

USE THIS SPACE to help you plan the order of service.

participant: *element of service:*

_____
_____
_____
_____
_____
_____
_____
_____
_____
_____
_____
_____
_____
_____
_____
_____
_____
_____
_____
_____

The LORD is my shepherd, I shall not be in want.
*   He makes me lie down in green pastures,*
he leads me beside quiet waters,
*   he restores my soul.*
He guides me in paths of righteousness
*   for his name's sake.*
Even though I walk
*   through the valley of the shadow of death,*
I will fear no evil,
*   for you are with me;*
your rod and your staff,
*   they comfort me.*

You prepare a table before me
*   in the presence of my enemies.*
You anoint my head with oil;
*   my cup overflows.*
Surely goodness and love will follow me
*   all the days of my life,*
and I will dwell in the house of the LORD
*   forever.*

PSALM 23
(THE HOLY BIBLE: NEW INTERNATIONAL VERSION)

Planning the interment (or alternate) service

A GRAVESIDE SERVICE is sometimes held either in addition to or instead of the service in a church or funeral home. Personal preference is again the rule of thumb on whether to have an interment service (or some other alternate); there are no set rules to follow.

Usually the interment service is shorter and simpler than the more elaborate and formal service in a church or funeral home. Sometimes at the interment a member of the military or a lodge organization will be honored with special elements of respect, such as presentation of the flag, gunnery salutes, and other rituals. These organizations have their own rules of conduct and etiquette for these presentations.

Some people include special elements in the interment service to make it more personal and memorable. (Again, refer to the end of this section for suggestions.)

place of interment: _____

day of week/date/time: _____

person(s) presiding: _____

    title, or relationship to deceased: _____

person presenting obituary: _____

    title, or relationship to deceased: _____

pall bearers: (indicate name and relationship to deceased)

_____

_____

_____

_____

_____

_____

_____

other participants: (indicate name, and form of participation)

_____

_____

_____

_____

_____

_____

_____

special wishes of the deceased:

_____

_____

_____

_____

_____

_____

On the next page is the outline of a simple, traditional interment
service.

Traditional Order of Interment Service

Johnson & Smith Funeral Home .... *Seating of Family*

Tom Jackson .... *Eulogy*

Don Phillips .... *Remarks to the Family*

Peter Ward .... *Prayer*

Family .... *Blessing of Flowers*

Johnson & Smith Funeral Home .... *Interment*

USE THIS SPACE to help you plan the order of service.

participant: *element of service:*

_____

_____

_____

_____

_____

_____

_____

_____

_____

_____

_____

_____

_____

_____

_____

_____

_____

Order of interment service

When we must be parted by death or distance, remember me with smiles and laughter, for that's how I'll be remembering you. If you can only remember me with tears, then don't remember me at all, for I would not cause you sorrow. Not now. No, not ever.

MARY HOLLINGSWORTH
IT'S A ONE-DERFUL LIFE!

Personalizing the service

WAYS TO PERSONALIZE a memorial or interment service are as numerous and varied as the people themselves. Here are elements the authors have experienced that made particular memorial services memorable, warm, and personal. Place a check mark by any of these ideas you would like to consider incorporating into the service you are planning.

____ Play the deceased's favorite musical tape before or after the actual service.

____ Allow various family members or friends to tell favorite tales or stories about the deceased as a part of the service. Happy, pleasant stories are particularly appropriate and appreciated at this time.

____ Place a special painting or photograph of the deceased at the head of the casket or in the hallway, and leave the casket closed during the service, to help those in attendance to remember the deceased as he or she looked while living.

____ Read something special the deceased wrote (perhaps a poem, or lines from a letter) that shows the deceased's positive view of life.

____ Read passages from the deceased's Bible or favorite book of poetry that have been underlined or highlighted.

____ Have a musical family member or friend sing a song with special meaning to the deceased or the family.

____ Display the deceased's handiwork (such as woodworking, crochet, painting, quilting, photographs) at the funeral facility.

____ Display a scrapbook that chronicles the life of the deceased.

____ Allow young children or grandchildren to participate in the service by reading from the deceased's Bible or favorite book, or by singing a song.

____ Play during the service a tape recording of the deceased singing a favorite song, talking to a friend, or reading from a favorite work.

____ Allow all those in attendance to sing together one of the deceased's favorite songs.

____ As a keepsake, provide a printed biography and photo of the deceased to those attending.

THANKS FOR THE MEMORIES

3

Acknowledgments

WHEN THE MEMORIAL SERVICE is over, you'll want to acknowledge with thanks the contributions of various people to the memory of the deceased. This section provides a place to record those contributions and your acknowledgment of thanks for them.

participant: _____

type of participation: _____

address: _____

city/state/zip: _____

date of acknowledgment: _____

participant: _____

type of participation: _____

address: _____

city/state/zip: _____

date of acknowledgment: _____

participant: _____

type of participation: _____

address: _____

city/state/zip: _____

date of acknowledgment: _____

participant: _____

type of participation: _____

address: _____

city/state/zip: _____

date of acknowledgment: _____

Memorial service participants

Memorial service participants
(continued)

participant: _____
type of participation: _____
address: _____
city/state/zip: _____
date of acknowledgment: _____

participant: _____
type of participation: _____
address: _____
city/state/zip: _____
date of acknowledgment: _____

participant: _____
type of participation: _____
address: _____
city/state/zip: _____
date of acknowledgment: _____

participant: _____
type of participation: _____
address: _____
city/state/zip: _____
date of acknowledgment: _____

participant: _____
type of participation: _____
address: _____
city/state/zip: _____
date of acknowledgment: _____

participant: _____
type of participation: _____
address: _____
city/state/zip: _____
date of acknowledgment: _____

participant: _____
type of participation: _____
address: _____
city/state/zip: _____
date of acknowledgment: _____

participant: _____

type of participation: _____

address: _____

city/state/zip: _____

date of acknowledgment: _____

participant: _____

type of participation: _____

address: _____

city/state/zip: _____

date of acknowledgment: _____

participant: _____

type of participation: _____

address: _____

city/state/zip: _____

date of acknowledgment: _____

participant: _____

type of participation: _____

address: _____

city/state/zip: _____

date of acknowledgment: _____

participant: _____

type of participation: _____

address: _____

city/state/zip: _____

date of acknowledgment: _____

participant: _____

type of participation: _____

address: _____

city/state/zip: _____

date of acknowledgment: _____

participant: _____

type of participation: _____

address: _____

city/state/zip: _____

date of acknowledgment: _____

Memorial service participants

(continued)

Floral tributes

ASK A CLOSE FRIEND or family member to remove the identification cards from all floral tributes. Ask her to record on the back of each card the type of flowers sent, and to give the cards to you later. The friend may want to coordinate with the funeral facility to decide the most appropriate time to perform the task. You may then want to transfer the information from the loose cards to these pages as a permanent record.

WHAT SHOULD I DO WITH THE FLOWERS? If a great many floral tributes are received, here are suggestions of appropriate ways to distribute them:

1. You may want some of the sprays to be taken to the interment service and left at the gravesite.
2. The closest relatives may want to choose one or more potted plants to take home with them as a living reminder of their loved one.
3. You might choose to donate a potted plant or two for display in the church of the deceased, or in your own church.
4. Homebound friends or relatives usually enjoy having pretty blooming or potted plants to cheer up their homes or convalescent room.
5. Rest homes and retirement centers are usually happy to receive plants and flowers.

Acknowledging floral tributes

received from: _____
type of flowers: _____
address: _____
city/state/zip: _____
date of acknowledgment: _____

received from: _____
type of flowers: _____
address: _____
city/state/zip: _____
date of acknowledgment: _____

received from: _____

type of flowers: _____

address: _____

city/state/zip: _____

date of acknowledgment: _____

received from: _____

type of flowers: _____

address: _____

city/state/zip: _____

date of acknowledgment: _____

received from: _____

type of flowers: _____

address: _____

city/state/zip: _____

date of acknowledgment: _____

received from: _____

type of flowers: _____

address: _____

city/state/zip: _____

date of acknowledgment: _____

received from: _____

type of flowers: _____

address: _____

city/state/zip: _____

date of acknowledgment: _____

received from: _____

type of flowers: _____

address: _____

city/state/zip: _____

date of acknowledgment: _____

received from: _____

type of flowers: _____

address: _____

city/state/zip: _____

date of acknowledgment: _____

received from: _____
type of flowers: _____
address: _____
city/state/zip: _____
date of acknowledgment: _____

received from: _____
type of flowers: _____
address: _____
city/state/zip: _____
date of acknowledgment: _____

received from: _____
type of flowers: _____
address: _____
city/state/zip: _____
date of acknowledgment: _____

received from: _____
type of flowers: _____
address: _____
city/state/zip: _____
date of acknowledgment: _____

received from: _____
type of flowers: _____
address: _____
city/state/zip: _____
date of acknowledgment: _____

received from: _____
type of flowers: _____
address: _____
city/state/zip: _____
date of acknowledgment: _____

received from: _____
type of flowers: _____
address: _____
city/state/zip: _____
date of acknowledgment: _____

received from: _____
type of flowers: _____
address: _____
city/state/zip: _____
date of acknowledgment: _____

received from: _____
type of flowers: _____
address: _____
city/state/zip: _____
date of acknowledgment: _____

received from: _____
type of flowers: _____
address: _____
city/state/zip: _____
date of acknowledgment: _____

received from: _____
type of flowers: _____
address: _____
city/state/zip: _____
date of acknowledgment: _____

received from: _____
type of flowers: _____
address: _____
city/state/zip: _____
date of acknowledgment: _____

received from: _____
type of flowers: _____
address: _____
city/state/zip: _____
date of acknowledgment: _____

received from: _____
type of flowers: _____
address: _____
city/state/zip: _____
date of acknowledgment: _____

received from: _____
type of flowers: _____
address: _____
city/state/zip: _____
date of acknowledgment: _____

received from: _____
type of flowers: _____
address: _____
city/state/zip: _____
date of acknowledgment: _____

received from: _____
type of flowers: _____
address: _____
city/state/zip: _____
date of acknowledgment: _____

received from: _____
type of flowers: _____
address: _____
city/state/zip: _____
date of acknowledgment: _____

received from: _____
type of flowers: _____
address: _____
city/state/zip: _____
date of acknowledgment: _____

received from: _____
type of flowers: _____
address: _____
city/state/zip: _____
date of acknowledgment: _____

received from: _____
type of flowers: _____
address: _____
city/state/zip: _____
date of acknowledgment: _____

FAMILIES (or the deceased, prior to death) often choose a favorite charity to which friends and others are asked to make contributions in lieu of floral tributes. Usually the receiving charity will acknowledge the gift both to the donor and to the family.

charity organization selected: _____

qualified by IRS as nonprofit charity? yes___ no___

address: _____

city/state/zip: _____

telephone number: _____

note: _____

donor: _____

amount: _____   received by (name of charity or organization):

_____

donor's address: _____

city/state/zip: _____

date of acknowledgment: _____

donor: _____

amount: _____   received by (name of charity or organization):

_____

donor's address: _____

city/state/zip: _____

date of acknowledgment: _____

donor: _____

amount: _____   received by (name of charity or organization):

_____

donor's address: _____

city/state/zip: _____

date of acknowledgment: _____

donor: _____

amount: _____   received by (name of charity or organization):

_____

donor's address: _____

city/state/zip: _____

date of acknowledgment: _____

Donors to acknowledge

(continued)

donor: _____

amount: _____ received by (name of charity or organization):

_____

donor's address: _____

city/state/zip: _____

date of acknowledgment: _____

donor: _____

amount: _____ received by (name of charity or organization):

_____

donor's address: _____

city/state/zip: _____

date of acknowledgment: _____

donor: _____

amount: _____ received by (name of charity or organization):

_____

donor's address: _____

city/state/zip: _____

date of acknowledgment: _____

donor: _____

amount: _____ received by (name of charity or organization):

_____

donor's address: _____

city/state/zip: _____

date of acknowledgment: _____

donor: _____

amount: _____ received by (name of charity or organization):

_____

donor's address: _____

city/state/zip: _____

date of acknowledgment: _____

donor: _____

amount: _____ received by (name of charity or organization):

_____

donor's address: _____

city/state/zip: _____

date of acknowledgment: _____

donor: _____

amount: _____ received by (name of charity or organization):

_____

donor's address: _____

city/state/zip: _____

date of acknowledgment: _____

donor: _____

amount: _____ received by (name of charity or organization):

_____

donor's address: _____

city/state/zip: _____

date of acknowledgment: _____

donor: _____

amount: _____ received by (name of charity or organization):

_____

donor's address: _____

city/state/zip: _____

date of acknowledgment: _____

donor: _____

amount: _____ received by (name of charity or organization):

_____

donor's address: _____

city/state/zip: _____

date of acknowledgment: _____

donor: _____

amount: _____ received by (name of charity or organization):

_____

donor's address: _____

city/state/zip: _____

date of acknowledgment: _____

donor: _____

amount: _____ received by (name of charity or organization):

_____

donor's address: _____

city/state/zip: _____

date of acknowledgment: _____

Other acknowl-edgments

name: _____
reason for acknowledgment: _____
address: _____
city/state/zip: _____
date of acknowledgment: _____

name: _____
reason for acknowledgment: _____
address: _____
city/state/zip: _____
date of acknowledgment: _____

name: _____
reason for acknowledgment: _____
address: _____
city/state/zip: _____
date of acknowledgment: _____

name: _____
reason for acknowledgment: _____
address: _____
city/state/zip: _____
date of acknowledgment: _____

name: _____
reason for acknowledgment: _____
address: _____
city/state/zip: _____
date of acknowledgment: _____

name: _____
reason for acknowledgment: _____
address: _____
city/state/zip: _____
date of acknowledgment: _____

name: _____
reason for acknowledgment: _____
address: _____
city/state/zip: _____
date of acknowledgment: _____

A RECORD OF LIFE

Planning for Posterity

4

> *Accolades and eulogies are pitiful attempts*
> *to say, "This person lived well." Far better*
> *to let a person's life speak for itself—*
> *children, work, service, love, laughter, hopes*
> *and dreams. These are the real person*
> *for these are the parts of life tried*
> *and triumphed. Don't let's say*
> *what made a person great;*
> *rather, let's look and smile.*
>
> MARY HOLLINGSWORTH

TIME HAS A MARVELOUS WAY of healing hurts and eliminating painful memories from the mind. Unfortunately, time dims our memory of important facts and information as well. This section of *The Grief Recovery Guide* will help you record vital and historical information about the deceased while these details are still clear in your mind.

We recommend that you double-check official documents (such as birth certificates and marriage licenses) for the information you will record in this section, to ensure absolute accuracy. And write *in ink* as a permanent record for the deceased's descendants and for your own future reference. (Some of this information can be copied from the obituary worksheet in Section 2, and perhaps enlarged upon on the following pages.)

FULL NAME: _____

Social Security number: _____

driver's license number: _____

residence at time of death—

address: _____

city/state/zip: _____

date of birth:_____

date of death: _____

age at death: _____ *years,* _____ *months,* _____ *days*

place of birth: *(include city, county or parish, state or province,*
*and country)*_____

Marriage

marital status at time of death: _____

name of spouse: _____

date of marriage: _____

previous marriage—

name of former spouse: _____

date of marriage: _____

date marriage dissolved: _____

reason of marriage dissolution: _____

Parents

father's full name: _____

father's birthplace: _____

mother's full name: _____

mother's birthplace: _____

Children

name: _____

son or daughter: _____ *birth date:* _____

birthplace: _____

name: _____

son or daughter: _____ *birth date:* _____

birthplace: _____

name: _____

son or daughter: _____ *birth date:* _____

birthplace: _____

name: _____

son or daughter: _____ *birth date:* _____

birthplace: _____

name: _____

son or daughter: _____ *birth date:* _____

birthplace: _____

name: _____

son or daughter: _____ *birth date:* _____

birthplace: _____

name: _____

son or daughter: _____ *birth date:* _____

birthplace: _____

name: _____

boy or girl: _____ *birth date:* _____

child of: _____

name: _____

boy or girl: _____ *birth date:* _____

child of: _____

name: _____

boy or girl: _____ *birth date:* _____

child of: _____

name: _____

boy or girl: _____ *birth date:* _____

child of: _____

name: _____

boy or girl: _____ *birth date:* _____

child of: _____

Grandchildren (continued)

name: _____

boy or girl: _____ birth date: _____

child of: _____

name: _____

boy or girl: _____ birth date: _____

child of: _____

name: _____

boy or girl: _____ birth date: _____

child of: _____

name: _____

boy or girl: _____ birth date: _____

child of: _____

name: _____

boy or girl: _____ birth date: _____

child of: _____

name: _____

boy or girl: _____ birth date: _____

child of: _____

name: _____

boy or girl: _____ birth date: _____

child of: _____

name: _____

boy or girl: _____ birth date: _____

child of: _____

name: _____

boy or girl: _____ birth date: _____

child of: _____

name: _____

boy or girl: _____ birth date: _____

child of: _____

usual occupation: _____

industry, profession, or business: _____

___*active* or ___*retired* at time of death

companies worked for *(indicate length of service)*:

_____

_____

_____

_____

notable achievements:

_____

_____

_____

_____

branch of service: _____

dates of service: *from:* _____ *to:* _____

rank achieved: _____

medals/honors received: _____

_____

veteran of which war(s): _____

places of service: _____

_____

(indicate all formal schooling, from early childhood on)

school: _____

location: _____

dates attended: *from:* _____ *to:* _____

school: _____

location: _____

dates attended: *from:* _____ *to:* _____

school: _____

location: _____

dates attended: *from:* _____ *to:* _____

Employ-ment

Military service

Education

Education (continued)

school: _____
location: _____
dates attended: *from:* _____ *to:* _____

school: _____
location: _____
dates attended: *from:* _____ *to:* _____

school: _____
location: _____
dates attended: *from:* _____ *to:* _____

school: _____
location: _____
dates attended: *from:* _____ *to:* _____

school: _____
location: _____
dates attended: *from:* _____ *to:* _____

high school diploma:
from *(name of school)*: _____
date of graduation: _____

degree earned: _____
from *(name of college or university)*: _____
date of graduation: _____

degree earned: _____
from: _____
date of graduation: _____

degree earned: _____
from: _____
date of graduation: _____

indicate office held, dates, and location)

Public offices held

_____

_____

_____

indicate organization name, dates of membership, and any special mem-
bership status or office held)

Lodges, clubs, associations

_____

_____

_____

_____

_____

indicate type of owner, from whom it was given, and the date given)

Special awards, honors, recognition

_____

_____

_____

_____

_____

_____

_____

Other items of special interest

_____

_____

_____

_____

_____

_____

Other items of
special interest
(continued)

A TIME TO REFOCUS

5

Beginning Again

> It was there — through the weeping rain,
> through the grey mourning clouds,
> through the salty tears blurring my vision —
> that I saw it:
> The sun winked at me.
> Oh, it was not a long, sunny smile;
> it was just a quick wink from behind a dark cloud.
> But then I knew: It was still there…
> the sun did still shine!
> It was then I determined to chase it —
> through the rain,
> past the clouds,
> in spite of my tears —
> until it smiled again happily for me…
> just for me.
>
> MARY HOLLINGSWORTH

WHAT IS GRIEF, AND WHY IS IT SO HARD?

Grief is the combination of sorrow, strong emotion, and resulting confusion that comes from losing someone important to you. Your volatile emotions are reactions to the loss, resulting in confusion that comes from being thrown off-balance in your life. It's like having the weight removed from the other side of your balance scales; it causes your side of the scales to drop to the bottom.

The
dynamics
of grief

5

This phenomenon explains why you may not be completely comforted at the time of loss, even if you have perfect assurance that your loved one is safe, happy, and in a better place. That knowledge helps, but sadness remains because you mourn not only for the one you've lost but for yourself as well. Don't be alarmed; it's a natural human response to losing a loved one.

ELEMENTS OF GRIEF

Experts in grief adjustment, such as Erich Lindemann and Colin Murray Parkes, suggest that the adjustment involves these things:

Shock and Numbness

Shock and numbness are very early feelings of grief that may last an hour, a day, a week, or even longer. In large part, these experiences are your body's ways of coping with the intense pain associated with your loss. You may find that this initial reaction includes moments of quietness followed by outbursts of sorrow. Shock is most intensely felt in cases of "sudden death."

Physical Sensations

You may find yourself experiencing one or more of the following physical reactions to the grief you are feeling:

1. Hollowness in the stomach
2. Tightness in the chest
3. A tightening of the throat
4. Irritability to noise
5. A sense of depersonalization — the feeling that nothing seems real, including yourself
6. Difficulty catching your breath
7. Muscle weakness
8. Lack of energy
9. Dry mouth

Searching

Don't be surprised if you find yourself searching for the one you have lost in "all the old familiar places." This desire arises out of your natural need to maintain the relationship you shared. This

> *To everything there is a season,*
> *and a time to every purpose under heaven:*
> *a time to be born, and a time to die;*
> *a time to plant, and a time to pluck up that*
> *which is planted...*
> *a time to weep, and a time to laugh;*
> *a time to mourn, and a time to dance...*
> *a time to get, and a time to lose;*
> *a time to keep, and a time to cast away...*
>
> ECCLESIASTES 3:1-6

need to search for your lost one may last as long as two years. It is normal.

The forms of searching you experience may range from dreams that seem as real as life itself, all the way to hallucinations caused by familiar sounds, smells, and sights. These hallucinations may come when you least expect them, causing you to be caught off-guard and unprepared. You might even feel it necessary to travel to areas where the lost one spent time. This, too, is a normal reaction to grief.

All these searchings are necessary for you because they help you confirm that the death of your loved one or special friend has actually occurred. Don't deny your need to search; it's a healthy step toward adjusting to your loss.

Subtle Sorrow

As you begin to realize the truth of your loss, you will settle into a less intense period of general sorrow and mourning. Your pain isn't as intense as it was before, yet it's always there. This "dulling" period of grief affects every area of your life. Food doesn't taste as good as it did before your loss. Colors aren't as bright as they were before. Jokes aren't as funny. Sleep isn't as deep. And energy isn't as readily available.

Your period of subtle sorrow may last for years. This, too, is normal in adjusting to grief. At certain times you may not particularly notice your grief. But at other times you'll feel as if you're covered in a blanket of pain. Hang on; you *are* making progress. As time goes on, times of peace will last longer, and times of emotional upheaval will come less often.

Moving from Chaos to Order

The final phase of grief adjustment involves your identifying the various roles the deceased played in your life, and then adjusting to the loss in each area. The disorganization you likely feel in your life comes in large part because you identify *too late* the tasks formerly performed by the deceased. This results in a lack of continuity in your life. The once familiar, comfortable patterns of life are suddenly replaced with unfamiliar chaos. It's only as you adjust one by one to the vacated roles that wholeness can return to you. New patterns can be established in each area, resulting in step-by-step adjustment.

SPECIAL FACTORS

You'll notice that these different phases of grief adjustment are described above in broad terms. You must have freedom to grieve in your own way. You may not react or adjust to grief in the same way as someone else you know, because each circumstance and relationship is unique.

Differences in the way people grieve may be caused by some of the factors below. Check the ones that apply to your relationship and situation.

1. What were the circumstances of death in your loss?
   ___ natural causes   ___ illness   ___ homicide
   ___ accident   ___ suicide

2. In what age bracket was the deceased?
   ___ a child   ___ a teenager   ___ a young adult
   ___ a middle-aged adult   ___ a senior adult

3. In what age bracket are you?
   ___ a teenager   ___ a young adult
   ___ a middle-aged adult   ___ a senior adult

4. Was there any prior warning of the death?
   ___ yes   ___ no

5. How would you describe your own personality?
    ___ dependent on my relationship with the deceased
    ___ independent in my relationship with the deceased
    ___ introvert   ___ extrovert

6. How would you describe your relationship with the deceased?
    ___ healthy   ___ unhealthy

All of the above factors will have an impact on your grief adjustment. List below any additional circumstances that you feel make your situation unique.

_____

_____

_____

_____

_____

_____

_____

_____

_____

_____

_____

_____

_____

_____

_____

_____

_____

WHILE THE NATURE of grief is different for each griever, there are some common denominators and experiences that almost all grievers experience. These include the first experiences of shock, numbness, denial, emotional outbursts, anger, fear, searchings, and disorganization; the deeper feelings of panic, loneliness, depression, guilt,and isolation; and on to experiences that reflect adjustment to grief — new relationships, new strengths, new patterns, hope, affirmation, and helping others.

The chart on the next page illustrates these typical experiences.

Finding yourself in the grief process

Work your way through this grief chart by focusing on your own loss experiences so far.

- ~~Cross out~~ experiences you remember *already having had.*
- <u>Underline</u> experiences you're *currently experiencing.*
- Place a check (✓) beside experiences you *haven't* had.

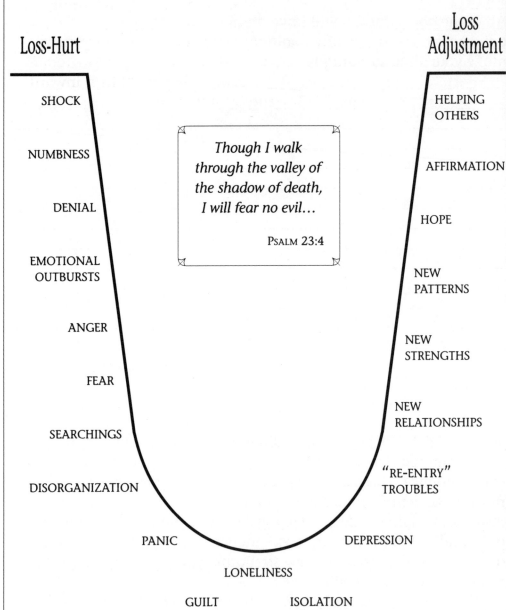

Loss-Hurt

Loss Adjustment

SHOCK

NUMBNESS

DENIAL

EMOTIONAL OUTBURSTS

ANGER

FEAR

SEARCHINGS

DISORGANIZATION

PANIC

LONELINESS

GUILT   ISOLATION

DEPRESSION

"RE-ENTRY" TROUBLES

NEW RELATIONSHIPS

NEW STRENGTHS

NEW PATTERNS

HOPE

AFFIRMATION

HELPING OTHERS

Though I walk through the valley of the shadow of death, I will fear no evil...

PSALM 23:4

There is no RIGHT *way to grieve — there is just* YOUR *way.*

RUSTY BERKUS
TO HEAL AGAIN

After working through the grief chart, answer these questions:

1. List ways you have freed yourself from being "stuck" in one
   phase.

   _____
   _____
   _____
   _____
   _____

2. Make some statements below to yourself about your own patterns of handling loss experiences. (Examples: "I turn inward
   instead of outward." "I internalize my anger.")

   _____
   _____
   _____
   _____
   _____
   _____
   _____
   _____
   _____

3. List the strengths you now have because of the grief you have
   experienced. (Examples: "I'm a survivor!" "I've learned
   empathy for others.")

   _____
   _____
   _____
   _____
   _____

4. What are ways these new strengths can be used to help others?

   _____
   _____
   _____
   _____
   _____
   _____
   _____

There's nothing wrong with grief. After all, grief is simply evidence that you loved someone special.

Performing your grief work

SAYING GOODBYE to someone special causes you grief. Your grief is not only caused by the desperate feelings connected with the death of someone you loved, but also by the lesser losses connected with your daily living. Whether large or small, a loss where an investment has been made always hurts and leaves a wound.

The degree of loss is not measured only in terms of the love shared through the various roles the deceased played in your life. The more roles the deceased filled, the more varied and complicated will be your adjustment. In other words, grief is not merely related to the *intensity* of love; it's also related to the *complexity* of your loss.

Here's a list of some identifiable roles people carry out for one another. Put a check mark by all the different roles the deceased played in your life.

```
__friend   __mechanic   __lover   __gardener
__companion __checkbook balancer   __parent
__motivator   __business partner   __playmate
__tax preparer   __spouse   __child   __brother
__sister   __provider   __audience   __stabilizer
__listener   __bill-payer   __confidant   __cook
__encourager   __accountability partner   __mentor
__source of inspiration   __teacher   __supporter
__counselor   __entertainer   __protector
__co-worker   __organizer
```

List below additional roles the deceased played for you:

_____

_____

_____

_____

_____

_____

_____

_____

Each role the deceased played in your life is in reality a separate loss to you. The more significant a particular role was in your life, the more intense the grief will be in that area. This is normal in the process of adjusting to grief.

Most survivors are unaware of all the roles a special person plays in their life until after the loss occurs. You may be discovering this now as well, and you may feel resentment at the deceased for vacating the roles he or she filled. This resentment by a griever often leads to guilt feelings. You may even feel angry at the deceased for dying. That's okay. It's normal to feel this way as you begin adjusting to all the new roles you must now fill yourself (or find others to fill).

This role-identification exercise will help you to see that your reaction to the loss you have suffered is more than mere sadness.

GRIEF IS A COMPLEX REACTION that fully involves your mind and emotions. It's especially important for you to realize that your loss has initiated a conflict between reality and what you want to exist. The *reality* is that you have lost someone important. What you *want* is for the deceased to continue being part of your life. What you are forced to face on one hand does battle with what you long for on the other.

Many grievers will actually refuse to believe that the death has occurred. They might even tell themselves, "I know that he (or she) is dead," even while doing something that proves they haven't really accepted that fact.

This inner battle is one of the complexities that creates confusion and makes the process of grieving so difficult for you.

Another inner conflict that often causes fear and confusion is sadness combined with one or more of the following. Check the different areas that relate to your own grief experiences:

__disbelief   __physical illness
__confusion   __guilt   __sleeplessness
__anger   __depression   __loneliness
__difficulty concentrating   __helplessness
__eating disorder   __emptiness   __lethargy
__loss of memory   __panic

Don't be alarmed if you feel a combination of many of these reactions. You're not losing your mind. You are reacting normally while your mind and body adjust to the fact of your loss.

Inner conflicts

Finding support

THE KEY to loss adjustment is *support*. Research shows that the following formulas prove to be true among people who have lost someone dear:

$$Loss + major\ change - support$$
$$= sickness,\ bitterness,\ alcoholism,\ drug\ abuse,\ isolation,\ etc.$$

$$Loss + major\ change + support$$
$$= growth\ and\ healing$$

Reviewing and defining the relationship you had with the deceased person is important, but merely *thinking* about these things is only a starting point. You need to share your feelings with at least one "significant other" person in your life — someone you trust. After you have identified the different roles the deceased played in your life, plan a time to communicate your feelings with a support person.

This person should be…

- someone who will listen without judging or analyzing you and your feelings.
- someone who will allow you to disclose all your feelings, the pleasant as well as the ugly.
- someone who will "enter your pain" — be understanding.
- someone who will provide an atmosphere in which you can grieve (or cry) without embarrassment.

Allow plenty of time for your meeting. You may even want to consider meeting with your friend regularly for a few weeks. Talking about the impact of your loss with an understanding friend helps you own the loss mentally and emotionally, which will open the door to easing the pain.

You may need to tell the support person(s) you select what kind of support you really need. Don't assume others will know how to give you the kind of support you want or require. Talk to them!

Here are some ways you may need them to support you. Put a check mark by the ones that you most need.

___ being a loving listener
___ helping you identify your feelings
___ helping you "own" your feelings
___ helping you express your feelings
___ being a long-term support

BECAUSE OF THE FLOOD of emotions that grief can bring about —
and the confusion that results — your loving listener may need to be
available to support you for six months or longer, with at least one
meeting per week.

Friends, family members, and well-wishers may try to hurry you
through your grief. They may even try to tell you how to react. Don't
let their good intentions upset you, even when you know their
approach is wrong for you. Just remember that each person grieves
in a unique way. Another person's pace will vary from yours. And
that's okay.

On the average it takes from one to five years to fully adjust to
the loss of a loved one. Some people will adjust quickly, others more
slowly.

The *kind* of death through which a loved one was lost is typically
a major factor in how long grief adjustment will last. The following
list is a general guide to the grief adjustment period relative to four
different kinds of death.

> __ natural death — *0-2 years*
> __ accidental death — *2-3 years*
> __ suicidal death — *3-4 years*
> __ homicidal death — *4-5 years*

The point is, don't rush yourself or allow yourself to be pushed
through the grief adjustment process. Take your time, as long as you
can see progress being made.

DON'T GET STUCK IN THE PROCESS

Sometimes grievers get "stuck" in a phase of loss adjustment.
Because of the pain related to your grief, you may find yourself
developing defense mechanisms — including *denial, anger,* and *guilt.*
These actually work against you, prolonging the grief process and
causing destructive complications. Make a commitment to yourself
not to get stuck in one of these defense mechanisms, as you explore
more about them on the following pages.

How long will it take?

Denial

MOST DENIAL takes place early in grief adjustment, and it may come in many forms. Put a check mark by any of these denial forms you see or hear yourself using, or that you've used before.

__ Denying the significance of your loss with statements (to yourself or to others) such as these: "We weren't really that close." "He wasn't really a good father." "I didn't really need her anyway."

__ Jettisoning, or throwing off, your grief feelings as being unimportant. This is a way of pretending the person you lost never existed, or that he or she did not have a significant presence in your life.

__ Refusing to accept the reality of the death, and instead adopting one of the following behaviors:

    __ retaining the person's room, workshop, wardrobe, etc.

    __ seeing the deceased in another person you know.

    __ pretending the deceased is alive. (This is not unusual for a short time, but it becomes destructive if allowed to continue.)

If you find yourself stuck, call your counselor or minister for help. Deliberately postponing or suppressing your grief does not make adjustment easier. In fact, it actually can make matters worse.

So don't hide your feelings or run from the pain. Allow your grief to happen. Reach out for help and support in your time of loss.

Anger

ALONG WITH SORROW, anger is a common emotion experienced during grief adjustment. The most frequent targets of their anger are represented in the following list. With check marks, indicate whether any of these have been targets of *your* anger in relation to your loss.

    __doctor   __nurse   __hospital   __minister
    __church   __neighbors   __friends   __children
    __parent(s)   __other family   __circumstances
    __God   __deceased   __yourself

If you've found yourself angry at anyone or anything else in relation to your loss, indicate this here:

_____

_____

_____

_____

Permitting yourself to be angry and express anger is difficult, especially if the environment in which you grew up did not allow anger, or frowned upon it. Anger, however, is often present whether we like it or not. You don't choose to be angry; you only choose whether you will allow yourself to express your anger.

There is, after all, a natural reason for your anger: You have lost someone you love, and you don't like it. If you want to be successful now in resolving this anger, you must acknowledge it.

Look back at the list of people toward whom you feel angry. In the following spaces (or on a separate sheet of paper), write each person a letter telling why you feel anger toward him in relation to your loss. (No one needs to see these letters except you; so go ahead and "tell it like it is.") *Expressing* your anger to yourself will help you understand it, and by understanding it you can begin to resolve it.

Dear _____,

    I feel anger towards you because ...

Sincerely,

Dear _____,

I feel anger towards you because ...

Sincerely,

Dear _____,

I feel anger towards you because ...

Sincerely,

ONE THING SHOULD EMERGE as you work through your anger: Some anger-triggering events are reasonable while others are not. You may even notice that in fact you're angry at no one specifically, but at everyone in general — and it's directed most often at those dearest and closest to you. That's just the way anger works.

Here are some exercises to help you work your way through your anger and continue on the road to grief adjustment. Take time to do these exercises carefully and thoroughly.

1. Recall and relive in your memory an anger-causing event related to your loss.

2. Concentrate on any feelings you may have connected to the person who caused that anger or event.

3. As if the person were there, carry on a dialogue with that person, saying out loud what is really on your heart and mind.

4. Next, respond to yourself for that person. Continue with this even though it feels strange. Try to put yourself in his place. Listen carefully to what he says back to you. For instance, he might say, "I'm sorry…" or "I didn't know…" or "I would change what happened, if I could." Keep the imaginary conversation going until the load of heavy feelings you feel toward that person is lightened. (Remember: Being angry does not mean you reject the person or object of your anger. By admitting your feelings openly and honestly, *you become free to decide the best way to handle your anger*.)

GUILT AND REGRET are common experiences of the griever. Whether appropriate or inappropriate, rational or irrational, feelings of guilt are often the key factors that keep people from adjusting and growing through the loss experience.

The things that produce guilt vary from griever to griever. Many of the most common factors are included in the following list. Put a check mark by any of the experiences or feelings which have meaning to you in your loss.

I should have...

___ provided better medical care.

___ allowed the operation.

___ chosen the right hospital.

___ selected a different treatment.

___ *(other:)* _____

I should have noticed he or she was...

___ sick.

___ sad.

___ depressed.

___ hurt.

___ lonely.

___ *(other:)* _____

I wish I had said...

_____

_____

_____

_____

I wish I had *not* said...

_____

_____

_____

_____

I wish I had done...

_____

_____

_____

_____

I wish I had *not* done...

_____

_____

_____

_____

I wish I had been…
        ___ kinder.
        ___ nicer.
        ___ more patient.
        ___ more attentive.
        ___ more understanding.
        ___ more observant.
        ___ more careful.
        ___ *(other:)* _____

I feel guilt when…
        ___ I am not experiencing an appropriate amount of sadness
              over my loss.
        ___ I am having a good time.
        ___ I find myself attracted to someone else.
        ___ I don't react the way others think I should.
        ___ I replace old habits and patterns with new.
        ___ I think about living without you.
        ___ *(other:)* _____

Guilt can come from any place or event imaginable. Its sources are endless. Some of these factors could have been altered while others could not, but guilt is experienced nonetheless. Guilt even comes from picking up the pieces and moving on to recovery. It's an inevitable part of the grieving process. However it does not need to control or destroy its victim. Guilt feelings can be managed by acknowledging them and choosing an appropriate response.

Instead of trying to determine whether you're "guilty," your focus needs to be, "What am I going to do about it?" Look back at what you checked on the list of guilt producers. What is an appropriate response in each situation?

If you truly could or should have done something different than you did, you may want to write the deceased a letter in the space provided on the next page. Tell him or her of your feelings. Read the letter aloud and "listen" for what his response to you might have been. Think of things the deceased would say if he or she were able — such things as, "I knew you cared," "I accept your apology," "It really wasn't your fault."

Dear _____,
   I'm feeling guilty because...

                                                            I love you,

In this letter to the loved one you've lost, you may even want to share any lessons you've learned as a result of his or her death. Those lessons might be something like these:

- Make every moment count with someone you love.
- Say the important things while you can.
- Live one day at a time.

What lessons have *you* learned?

_____
_____
_____
_____
_____
_____
_____
_____
_____
_____
_____
_____
_____

An *appropriate* response to guilt is one that allows you to...
- acknowledge the past — that which really happened.
- accept the consequences, and apologize if necessary.
- learn from past mistakes.
- grow toward the future, based on your newly acquired knowledge.

An *inappropriate* response to guilt is one which may...
- allow your guilt feelings to continually motivate your present behavior.
- lock you into living in the past, rather than letting you live in the present.
- cause you to feel badly in order to punish yourself.
- make you blame yourself for actions you could not control.

Grief is natural — so let it happen, and then move on naturally to the rest of your fulfilling life.

- To grieve properly is not to forget the lost one, for death does not end a relationship. Instead, proper grief lets go of the one lost so that new relationships and attachments can be made.
- Healthy grieving allows room for both old memories and new dreams to exist together. Remembering fondly the events and people of our past while continuing to build new relationships with new experiences is what life's all about.
- Adjustment to loss cannot be made instantly. It will come only through a commitment to living your life to the fullest, one day at a time. Experience all the joy, sadness, sorrow, peace, quietness, anger and forgiveness that life has to offer.
- Today's pain has a vital purpose, allowing you to say goodbye to living in the past so you can live in the present and build a healthy future.
- Don't rush through your grief — but commit to not getting stuck either.

Precious memories, precious dreams

LIFE IS MADE of precious memories and precious dreams. That's because our experiences are bundled up into what we call our past, and our hopes are bundled up into what we call our future. That's just how life is intended to be. It is right and good.

On the next few pages you can write down your favorite memories of the deceased. Record freely your wonderful feelings. Write about funny and happy times together. Glue photographs of happy events on the pages. Record gentle, sweet times, as well as difficult but growing times. Laugh and cry as you put together this permanent account of the beautiful moments you shared with the precious one you've now lost.

> *Precious memories, how they linger,*
> *How they ever flood my soul.*
> *In the stillness of the midnight,*
> *Precious sacred scenes unfold.*
>
> A. B. F. WRIGHT

I remember when...

Some of our
happiest
times
were...

Bridges we built over troubled waters...

Happenings and holidays...

I'll never forget...

Waves of Memory

An ocean of your memories
Slaps in waves upon
The shores of my mind...
Some gently washing away
Footprints of past lonely days
And leaving clear sands of sweet remembrance;
Some crashing fiercely against
Emotional boulders and gouging
Crevices of sorrow in my soul.

I stroll the beach alone
Searching for you
In the caves, among the rocks, on lofty craigs
Of my heart
And find you ever there,
Quietly awaiting my return
In our peaceful lagoon of love,
As the tide of memory swirls in.

MARY HOLLINGSWORTH

TIME TO MOVE ON

Recording Your Progress

6

SOMETIMES our wonderful memories try to dominate our dreams and push them aside. When that happens, it's time to take corrective action to put our precious memories in their proper place. Memories shackle us to what *was*; dreams pull us forward toward what *can be.*

GRIEVING IS NOT a constant climb with easily definable steps that are reached once, then left behind. Instead the process is often confusing, and sometimes the same stages of grief must be dealt with several times — two steps forward, one step back.

Journaling

Keeping a personal journal is one of the most helpful tools you can use to record and review your progress in grief adjustment. Expert counselors recognize journaling as one of the most beneficial things a hurting person can do to find healing. Your journal can become living proof that you are indeed making progress, even when you may not *feel* you're going forward.

Your journal is private; no one else needs to read it. Therefore, spelling and grammar are not important. What *is* important is that you have a place to say what you really feel. Your journal is a safe haven where you can feel, own, express, and examine your grief feelings — feelings that may often confuse, discourage, and defeat.

Through your journal you'll be able to look back and see the development of a new you. You'll recognize that adjustment to your loss *is* possible, and that healing is coming, though it takes time.

Some suggestions:

1. Most people find it helpful to make time every day to write at least a short paragraph in their journal. At the end of each week they review what they have written to see small steps of progress toward grief adjustment. Writing at least a line or two every day is the most effective way to journal.

2. Other people write in their journal a couple of times each week, reviewing it at the end of each week and at the end of each month.

3. Due to daily schedule problems or a shortage of discipline or energy, some people write in their journal only once a week, but usually for a longer period of time. (In the opinion of most experts, journaling must be done *at least* once a week to be effective.)

Journal starters

IF YOU HAVE TROUBLE getting started when you come to your journal to write, look over the list below of suggested beginnings. Find one that fits what you are feeling or need to express and use it to "jump-start" your journaling for that day.

1. My biggest struggle right now is…
2. The thing that really gets me down is…
3. The worst thing about my loss is…
4. When I feel lonely…
5. The thing I most fear is…
6. The most important thing I've learned…
7. The thing that keeps me from moving on is…
8. I seem to cry most when…
9. I dreamed last night…
10. I heard a song that reminded me of…
11. A new person I've come to appreciate is…
12. I get angry when…
13. Part of the past that keeps haunting me is…
14. What I've learned from the past is…
15. Guilt feelings seem to come most when…
16. The experiences I miss the most are…
17. New experiences I enjoy the most are…
18. The changes I least and most like are…

19. My feelings sometimes confuse me because…
20. I smelled a smell or saw a sight today that reminded me of…
21. A new hope I found today is…
22. New strengths I've developed since my loss are…
23. I feel close to God today because…
24. I am angry at God today because…
25. For me to find and have balance, I…
26. I got a call or letter from a friend today that…
27. My friend, _____, had a loss today, and I…

If one of these "starters" doesn't fit, then write about what you *are* feeling. You could start with just one word — "misery," "longing," "hope," or whatever — then describe that feeling with phrases or sentences. If you need to, cry as your write — but keep writing until there is nothing more to say about that feeling.

Your journal is yours to say and feel what's in your heart and mind. It's your way of crystallizing the feelings of loss. Dealing with your feelings one at a time in a written, tangible form is a good way to "own" those feelings and respond to them in an organized way. Grief is a whole tangle of feelings, and writing them down is a great way to isolate and adjust to each one.

Monitor what you write. When you begin to see yourself writing more about what is happening *today* and less about the one you have lost, you'll know that healing and adjustment are indeed taking place, though it may seem painfully slow. Look for signs of progress.

It's *your* journal; use it for your own benefit. Other than your "loving listener," your journal will be the most important tool you have for healthy adjustment to your grief.

When you have used up all the pages included here, you may wish to continue journaling in a notebook or blank book that you can purchase at your bookstore.

MY
GRIEF
ADJUSTMENT
JOURNAL

date

_____
_____
_____
_____
_____
_____
_____
_____
_____
_____
_____

date

_____
_____
_____
_____
_____
_____
_____
_____
_____
_____
_____

date

_____
_____
_____
_____
_____
_____
_____
_____
_____
_____
_____
_____

date

_____
_____
_____
_____
_____
_____
_____
_____
_____
_____
_____
_____
_____

date

_____
_____
_____
_____
_____
_____
_____
_____
_____
_____
_____
_____

date

_____
_____
_____
_____
_____
_____
_____
_____
_____
_____
_____

date

_____
_____
_____
_____
_____
_____
_____
_____
_____
_____
_____

date

_____
_____
_____
_____
_____
_____
_____
_____
_____
_____
_____

date

date

date

date _____

_____

_____

_____

_____

_____

_____

_____

_____

_____

_____

_____

date _____

_____

_____

_____

_____

_____

_____

_____

_____

_____

_____

_____

date _____

_____

_____

_____

_____

_____

_____

_____

_____

_____

_____

_____

date

_____
_____
_____
_____
_____
_____
_____
_____
_____
_____

date

_____
_____
_____
_____
_____
_____
_____
_____
_____
_____
_____

date

_____
_____
_____
_____
_____
_____
_____
_____
_____
_____

date
_____

_____
_____
_____
_____
_____
_____
_____
_____
_____

date
_____

_____
_____
_____
_____
_____
_____
_____
_____
_____

date
_____

_____
_____
_____
_____
_____
_____
_____
_____
_____

date

date

date

date

date

date

My Grief Adjustment Journal

date

date

date

date _____

_____
_____
_____
_____
_____
_____
_____
_____
_____
_____
_____

date _____

_____
_____
_____
_____
_____
_____
_____
_____
_____
_____
_____

date _____

_____
_____
_____
_____
_____
_____
_____
_____
_____
_____
_____

My Grief Adjustment Journal

date

date

date

My Grief Adjustment Journal

date
_____

_____
_____
_____
_____
_____
_____
_____
_____
_____
_____
_____
_____

date
_____

_____
_____
_____
_____
_____
_____
_____
_____
_____
_____
_____
_____

date
_____

_____
_____
_____
_____
_____
_____
_____
_____
_____
_____
_____
_____

CHOOSING LIFE

7

Getting Organized to Survive

> *No greater tragedy can be found than that of a soul crying out, "It's not fair!" and allowing the cold waters of cynicism to overflow and drown him. On the other hand, no greater victory can be won than by the person who has been plunged into those same waters and says, "I cannot feel the bottom, but I'll swim until I can!"*
>
> DORIS E. DOUGHERTY

SURVIVING THE LOSS of someone dear to you is the result of a range of conscious choices you must make. It means choosing dreams over memories. It means choosing hope over despair. It is, in fact, a choice for life.

When the choice for life has been made, you must get organized to survive the ups and downs you will experience during the period of grief adjustment. Organizing yourself involves planning ahead, taking care of business, and being prepared to meet the challenges of a new and different life. It involves setting realistic goals, both short-term and long-term. Mostly, it requires determination and hard work on your part to take life by the shoulders and give it a good shake.

Here are some things to recognize and consider as you begin to get organized to survive and adjust to your loss:

1. Set your *own* goals, rather than goals others provide for you.
2. Believe that you will not always feel as you do now. Healing

Do's and don'ts for survival

takes time — much more time than you will want it to take — but it will come.

3. Make decisions carefully...one at a time. Try not to make major decisions too soon. Determine which decisions *must* be made quickly and which ones can be delayed until later.

4. Find or build a support network of people who understand your loss and accept you in your current state of grief.

5. Be good to yourself. Go to the movies, read a good book, take a trip to somewhere you've always wanted to go, unplug the phone and relax in a hot tub for an hour, treat yourself to a meal in a fancy restaurant.

6. Get into a healthy routine of daily and weekly activities. Eat regularly, go to work, do volunteer work, exercise, and so on.

7. Be aware of new strengths you gain as time goes by.

8. Think about your relationship to the deceased in a positive way. What good things did you bring to the relationship?

9. Protect your personal feelings, priorities, and values. Refuse invitations to events or social outings that conflict with those priorities and values.

10. Accept help graciously when you need it.

11. Use your loss crisis as a stepping stone to a new life experience.

12. Help yourself grow (you're the only one who can) by talking about your desires and your limitations, and by making your requests known to others.

13. Show appreciation for your friends who become "loving listeners" and affirm your growth. Don't just share your grief with those persons; talk about other things too.

14. Remind yourself that growth is a lifelong process, and grief is just one more step toward maturity.

TEN DON'TS — Here are pitfalls to avoid in the grief-adjustment process. Put check marks by anything in this list that you find yourself violating.

__ Don't withdraw totally from life and your friends.
__ Don't deny or suppress your feelings of grief.
__ Don't back away from new relationships.
__ Don't put yourself down for feeling vulnerable.
__ Don't be surprised if you experience sudden physical problems.

- __ Don't dwell on the unfairness of your loss.
- __ Don't base new relationships entirely on trying to please the other person.
- __ Don't rush into remarriage.
- __ Don't get too upset when people say either nothing or "the wrong thing" to you about your loss. Their hearts are right, but their judgment is faulty.
- __ Don't feel guilty about sometimes being away from your children.

ADAPTED FROM *BEGINNING AGAIN: THE CHALLENGE OF THE FORMERLY MARRIED* BY NANCY POTTS (DAVID C. COOK PUBLISHING COMPANY, ELGIN, IL).

TEN DO'S — Now, flip the coin over and identify the positive things you are doing. Put check marks by anything in this list of helpful activities that you find yourself doing.

- __ Live one day at a time — today.
- __ Seek help. Find or build a support network. No one grieves properly alone.
- __ Grieve at your own pace. Take your time.
- __ Accept the reality of your loss.
- __ Talk to someone else about your feelings, even those hard-to-express feelings.
- __ Write in your Grief Adjustment Journal regularly. It provides a yardstick for measuring your progress.
- __ Allow yourself to have bad days and moments. Grief adjustment is not a steady, uphill climb.
- __ Plan ahead for holidays or special days, such as anniversaries. Have your support group handy, just in case you need them. It sometimes helps to plan a full day, or nothing at all, depending on your needs.
- __ Cry when you feel like it. Crying is your body's way of releasing your tension, stress, anger, fear, loss and longing. It's normal and healthful.
- __ Reach out to others who need to learn and grow as you have.

Never look at what you have lost. Look at what you have left.

ROBERT SCHULLER

Becoming active again

THE MOST DIFFICULT PHASE of grieving is getting organized to survive. It generally comes when you are least prepared to accomplish the task. The shock of your loss, combined with your sorrow and loneliness, causes you to feel lethargic, and that lack of energy comes when energy is needed most.

Inactivity feels good at first. The need to relax and sleep at times is overwhelming, even though good, restful sleep seems like an impossibility. On a short-term basis, this idle, non-focused reaction is okay, but there comes a time when you must take that first step of becoming active again and getting organized to survive — or else the idleness will begin working against you.

The first step is always the hardest, but it's necessary just the same. Once activity has been started, a strategy for growth can be planned. It's during this time of potential growth that you can create new directions, establish new values, develop inner resources, and create your own set of techniques for life management.

Time frames for survival

TO ACCOMPLISH your personal adjustment to loss, you may want to use these three time frames in thinking of the immediate future:

TIME PERIOD:	YOUR FOCUS:
from the time of loss through one month afterward	**Getting Started** *Today*
one month through six months afterward	**Short-Term Goals**
six months through two years afterward	**Long-Term Goals**

Getting organized in this way provides a workable framework from which to see both where you've been and where you're going. *(See the planning calendars at the end of this section. These are organized according to the three time frames outlined above.)*

Caution: Be realistic about expectations you set for yourself. Some goals can be reached easily, but others may take more time and effort. Make sure your goals are reachable and logical *for you.* It's not a realistic expectation that all the pain will be gone in six months.

THE FIRST PHASE of adjustment, which generally lasts from the date of loss through about the first month afterward, can be lived through successfully by following certain truths. These truths have been affirmed thousands of times by all the people before you who have encountered and survived the kind of grief you are now suffering. Believe them. Trust them. Follow them to begin your adjustment.

GRIEVE EARLY AND INTENSELY — Being strong for others is an unfair expectation people often place on themselves. Don't operate on the premise that the right approach is getting back to normal so that others can be comfortable around you. The fact that you are grieving is a sign that you are healing and growing as a person. King Solomon, whom the Bible calls the wisest man who ever lived, said, "There is a time for everything under heaven...a time to *mourn* and a time to *dance*...." The earlier you intensely grieve, the sooner you will adjust.

LIVE ONE DAY AT A TIME — This principle is healthy for people at all times in life, but it is particularly important to anyone who has recently suffered a significant loss. Because of the role adjustments imposed by your loss, there may be many new and unfamiliar tasks before you, and you feel the need to accomplish everything as quickly as possible. This can cause you to feel overwhelmed. Resist the temptation to accomplish everything too soon. Instead, focus only on your own grief and personal necessities.

POSTPONE AS MANY MAJOR DECISIONS AS YOU — To make good decisions, you need a clear thinking process. This is most difficult after the shock of a significant loss. Therefore we encourage you at this point to make only the decisions that are absolutely necessary. You may be surprised at how many decisions can be postponed until you regain your balance and can think through them clearly. Simply decide *not* to decide right now.

KEEP IT SIMPLE AND UNCOMPLICATED — At the beginning of each day, write out your list of goals on the calendar pages provided in this section. Focus only on the things you must do today. Keep the list simple so you can experience success early in the adjustment process. When you have completed an item on your list of goals for today, mark it off. You have succeeded. What's important here is movement, even if it's small or slow. The real work will come in time. So make it through today, and let tomorrow's worries take care of themselves.

Sample Goals for Today
__ call tailor
__ pick up cleaning
__ go to grocery store
__ prepare dinner
__ write in journal

First-month goals — legal & financial

HERE ARE SUGGESTIONS of legal and financial tasks that are best accomplished within the first month following your loss. To keep from overlooking them, you may wish to write them on your planning calendar at the end of this section. (As needed, refer to the legal planning suggestions in Section 9 of this book.)

DEATH CERTIFICATE — Order at least a dozen certified copies of the death certificate from the funeral director (or, if that's not applicable, from the county or parish clerk's office). These will usually cost about five dollars each. A dozen probably sounds like a lot, but you will need them often as you settle the deceased's affairs. For instance, a certified copy of the death certificate is usually required to claim death benefits on all insurance policies. They are also needed for Social Security records and for renaming joint assets, such as bank accounts.

THE WILL — Within the first two weeks after your loss, have your attorney review the will, if there is one, and file it in probate court if required by law. Probating a will can take several months, depending on the estate's complexity and various state laws; so it's best to get the process started as quickly as possible.

OTHER DOCUMENTS — Such documents as a birth certificate, marriage certificate, brokerage statements, insurance policies and others may also need to be gathered for claiming death benefits and for valuing the estate of the deceased. Your attorney can help you sort out any problems.

DEATH BENEFITS — Death benefits may be available in many different forms, depending on the deceased's estate planning. Generally, you will need to contact the following people or agencies to claim death benefits:

FINANCIAL ADVISER — Did the deceased have a financial adviser who handled his or her investments and other financial affairs? If so, contact that person first. The financial adviser will likely have a record of the deceased's various investments and can tell you under which ones a death benefit is probable. If there is no financial adviser, however, you will need to contact each person directly.

financial adviser's name: _____

name: _____

address: _____

city/state/zip: _____

telephone number: _____

EMPLOYER —

deceased's employer: _____

personnel benefits representative: _____

deceased's employee I.D. number: _____

company: _____

employer's address: _____

city/state/zip: _____

telephone number: _____

Ask the employer's representative if the deceased was entitled to any of these possible benefits through the company:

__ life insurance? *amount:* _____
   beneficiary: _____
__ accidental death benefit? *benefit:* _____
__ retirement program? _____
__ company stock/investment plan? _____
__ company credit union? _____
__ other benefits? _____

_____

_____

INSURANCE AGENT — Did the deceased have an "Agent of Record" who handled all of his or her various insurance investments? If so, contact that person first to confirm the list of insurance policies owned by the deceased and under which a benefit may be payable.

Agent of Record: _____

company: _____

address: _____

city/state/zip: _____

telephone number: _____

If there is no Agent of Record and you have no list of accumulated insurance investments for the deceased, it will be necessary to locate copies of existing insurance policies among the deceased's important papers. Then contact each insurance company — or, if you prefer, have your attorney contact them for you.

For convenience and quick reference, you may wish to list those policies in the spaces below.

• insurance company: _____

agent to contact: _____

address: _____

city/state/zip: _____

telephone number: _____

policy number: _____

name of insured: _____

type of policy: _____

cash value of policy: _____

claim requirements: _____

_____

_____

_____

date contacted: _____

• insurance company: _____

agent to contact: _____

address: _____

city/state/zip: _____

telephone number: _____

policy number: _____

name of insured: _____

type of policy: _____

cash value of policy: _____

claim requirements: _____

_____

_____

_____

date contacted: _____

• insurance company: _____

agent to contact: _____

address: _____

city/state/zip: _____

telephone number: _____

policy number: _____

name of insured: _____

type of policy: _____

cash value of policy: _____

claim requirements: _____

_____

_____

_____

date contacted: _____

• insurance company: _____

agent to contact: _____

address: _____

city/state/zip: _____

telephone number: _____

policy number: _____

name of insured: _____

type of policy: _____

cash value of policy: _____

claim requirements: _____

_____

_____

_____

date contacted: _____

• insurance company: _____

agent to contact: _____

address: _____

city/state/zip: _____

telephone number: _____

policy number: _____

name of insured: _____

type of policy: _____

cash value of policy: _____

claim requirements: _____

_____

_____

_____

date contacted: _____

• insurance company: _____

agent to contact: _____

address: _____

city/state/zip: _____

telephone number: _____

policy number: _____

name of insured: _____

type of policy: _____

cash value of policy: _____

claim requirements: _____

_____

_____

_____

date contacted: _____

SOCIAL SECURITY REPRESENTATIVE — You can find your local Social Security office in your telephone book's *Yellow Pages*. Give this agency a call to determine what benefits are available in the deceased's account.

Social Security representative: _____

office address: _____

city/state/zip: _____

telephone number: _____

deceased's Social Security number: _____

benefits available: _____

_____

claim requirements: _____

_____

_____

date contacted: _____

BANKERS — Other death benefits may be available in connection with bank investments of the deceased, such as savings accounts, trust funds, secured deposits, safe deposit boxes, and others. These may or may not all be concentrated in one banking facility. Again, you may need to check through the deceased's important papers to find such things as bank books, deposit certificates, bonds, safe deposit box keys, and other documents. Contact the deceased's banker(s) to determine what steps are necessary to claim the benefits available.

• bank name: _____

banker's name: _____

address: _____

city/state/zip: _____

telephone number: _____

date contacted: _____

account number: _____

    type of account: _____

    account held jointly? *yes*___ *no*___

    named beneficiary: _____

    benefit available: _____

    claim requirements: _____

    _____

    type of account: _____

    account held jointly? *yes*___ *no*___

    named beneficiary: _____

    benefit available: _____

    claim requirements: _____

    _____

• bank name: _____

banker's name: _____

address: _____

city/state/zip: _____

telephone number: _____

date contacted: _____

account number: _____

    type of account: _____

    account held jointly? *yes*___ *no*___

    named beneficiary: _____

    benefit available: _____

    claim requirements: _____

    _____

    type of account: _____

    account held jointly? *yes*___ *no*___

    named beneficiary: _____

    benefit available: _____

    claim requirements: _____

    _____

• bank name: _____

banker's name: _____

address: _____

city/state/zip: _____

telephone number: _____

date contacted: _____

account number: _____

    type of account: _____

    account held jointly? *yes*___ *no*___

    named beneficiary: _____

    benefit available: _____

    claim requirements: _____

    _____

AFTER THE FIRST MONTH, the shock is probably over, the reality of loss is beginning to set in, and everyone seems to have adjusted to the loss — except you. This second period in the grief-adjustment process — typically beginning after the first month and continuing until the sixth month — can be the loneliest of all, because family and friends have returned to their normal patterns of life. The support that was present in the first few days and weeks begins to diminish. It's not because others *don't* care, but because they forget how much you *do* care.

This time frame is important because, to a large degree, adjustment is based on what you do or don't do during this period. Goals need to be formed based on what you *want* to do or be. Invest *now* in those goals, as you balance new beginnings with fond remembrances. No one can find the right balance and set the right goals for you; you must do it for yourself. And the time to get started is now.

Here are the tasks that characterize this phase of adjustment:

BUILD YOUR SUPPORT NETWORK, AND USE IT — The number one key to emotional adjustment is having at least one friend with whom to share what you are feeling. Ideally you will have *more* than one, so that the support available to you will multiply. It may be that you will want to locate a support group to help you through your grief. Start by contacting hospitals or mental health centers for ongoing support groups. *The worst mistake you can make is to do nothing.* People don't know how to help unless you tell them. They can't read your mind. They may even assume you're doing fine when you really need help. Talk to them.

ASSESS YOUR PRESENT AND FUTURE GOALS AND PLANS — The adjustments required following a loss are resented in large part because they are being forced. We would rather have our loved one back than face the future alone. Since that can't happen, we are left to decide what to do next.

In reality, this period is full of opportunities — opportunities to start over. But this time, you can make the choices *you* want to make. You might choose to...

- get a new job.
- go back to school.

- move.
- change your hairstyle and wardrobe.
- learn a new language.
- travel.
- be in an exercise class.
- take up a new hobby.
- make new friends.

Using this list as a beginning place, answer the following questions.

1. If you could do anything you wanted to do with the rest of your life, what would that be? (Make a list of your dreams.)

_____

_____

_____

_____

_____

_____

_____

_____

_____

_____

_____

_____

_____

_____

2. Make a list of things keeping you from achieving your dreams.

_____

_____

_____

_____

_____

_____

_____

_____

_____

_____

_____

_____

3. Make a list of the assets (talents, skills, resources, time, etc.) you possess that will enable you to achieve your dreams.

_____

_____

_____

_____

_____

_____

_____

_____

_____

_____

_____

_____

Use this exercise to help you explore your ideals. The short-term period is for exploring the kinds of things you would enjoy doing. Go ahead and get started. If you find you don't enjoy a new activity as much as you thought, stop it and try something else. Your loss, as painful as it is, has given you an opportunity to assess your life and make adjustments if you choose. It's perfectly normal — and it's okay — for you to want to do something new and exciting with your life. And you can.

Legal and financial goals for the first six months

AS YOU CONTINUE to work through your grief during these early months after your loss, you will need to make the following legal and financial adjustments. (As needed, refer to the legal planning suggestions in Section 9 of this book.) Put a check mark by each of these areas as you accomplish them:

— Update your own will.

Change the beneficiary designations (where necessary) on:
__ insurance policies
__ retirement plans
__ savings accounts
__ deeds
__ bonds and securities
__ other investment vehicles: _____
_____

Change the names on:
__ joint-billing accounts
__ credit cards
__ banking accounts
__ deeds
__ car titles
__ others: _____
_____

If you are serving as the executor or administrator of the deceased's estate, notify creditors and satisfy debts as required by the probate laws of your state. (*Warning:* Sending phony debt notices to the family of persons deceased is a favorite con game. Refer any suspicious bills to your attorney.)

THE THIRD MAJOR PERIOD in grief adjustment (six months to two years) is controlled by the desire to find behavior that is appropriate, while launching out into new areas that will eventually create a new you. You find yourself asking, How should I dress, talk, act, respond? If I do grow in my adjustment, what will everyone think? Will they think I'm selfish, moving on without a thought for my lost loved one? What is appropriate behavior for a widow or widower (or a parent who has lost a child, or a child who has lost a parent)?

Here are some of the issues to be resolved:

IDENTITY — Are you half a person, or are you a complete person who has suffered a loss and is now trying to adjust? An exercise to help you focus on your identity and the changes that have occurred is this: In the list below, check each relationship or task that formed the basis of *your* whole identity *prior* to your loss. Add others in the spaces provided. These should relate to your entire being, not just your relationship to the deceased.

__parent __lover __mate/spouse __comedian
__encourager __listener __supporter __friend __child
__employer __employee __cook __nurse
others: _____ _____

_____ _____ _____

_____ _____

Now, from this list, mark out any relationships or tasks that no longer exist based on your loss (taking into account the time that has transpired and the adjustments that have been made).

Notice that your self-image may have *changed* based on role adjustment, but it has not been *altered completely*. No matter how many roles and relationships you lost, there are others that have remained constant. And now new roles and relationships have been formed.

That's the process of life — growth and change.

Try to answer these two questions for yourself as completely and candidly as you can:

Who am I? _____

_____

_____

_____

_____

_____

_____

_____

_____

_____

Who would I like to become? _____

_____

_____

_____

_____

_____

_____

_____

_____

_____

_____

In this third major time frame in the grief-adjustment process, the rule is this: *Don't quit until you are satisfied with yourself.*

RELATIONSHIPS — Any time a significant loss occurs, the first pains come from the void left by loss in relationship. Intimacy, love, bonding, camaraderie, friendship — these things don't happen instantly or even painlessly. To lose a relationship where a large investment has been made creates a huge void in your life. Adjustment to that void is never easy.

If forming new relationships has been particularly tough, you might try doing things you enjoy — going to church, bowling, taking art classes, going to museums or plays. The advantage this gives you is that it automatically places you with people who have interests in common with you. Few relationships are formed because you set out to have a relationship. They are formed instead by participating in things you enjoy and sharing those experiences with others.

HARD WORK — Establishing new patterns of lifestyle is, in most cases, not a glorious affair. Instead, the time is full of uncertainty as you begin growing in self-confidence by mastering new tasks and patterns. Joy comes from being able to look back and realize you've really made progress — in most cases, lots of it. New coping skills have emerged, new relationships formed. Plans have been made and achieved.

None of these accomplishments are earth-shattering when viewed alone, but when combined with everything else, you can say, "I'm a survivor!" The strength that comes from this knowledge will carry you on.

Here are additional areas of hard work to be done as your grief adjustment continues:

__ Continue to write each day in your Journal.

__ Continue to grieve openly when appropriate occasions arise. Resist feeling guilty because you think you should be through grieving by now. Remember that grief is a long-term proposition. It's still okay to hurt, even if the intensity is not as high.

__ When you are able, find ways to say goodbye to your lost one. Closure will come in time and cannot be forced. Goodbyes may be done in a direct way or simply by adjusting from living in the past to the present. Be open to ways you might find to say goodbye.

Legal and financial goals — six months to two years

NOW THAT the first frantic months since your loss have passed, begin working on more long-term legal and financial considerations. (Again, refer as needed to the legal planning suggestions in Section 9.)

ESTATE TAXES — If you are the executor or administrator of the deceased's estate, you must pay any taxes the estate owes. You are required to file federal estate taxes within nine months of the death if the estate is above a certain amount. Ask your attorney about this.

If the estate remains open, you must pay the estate's annual income taxes.

MAKING POSTPONED DECISIONS — Now is the time to begin making those decisions you postponed in the early days of your loss. Take your time. Seek professional advice when necessary. Think long-range. And move cautiously as you begin to decide such things as these:

1. Should I sell the house? *yes__ no__*
2. How should I invest my money? _____
   _____
3. Should I make a career move? *yes__ no__*
4. Should I go back to school? *yes__ no__*

What other decisions have you postponed until now? You may want to list them below as reminders to yourself.

_____
_____
_____
_____
_____
_____
_____
_____

PLANNING CALENDARS

- "Goals for Today"
  (for daily planning in the first month)

- full-page monthly calendars
  for the first six months

- smaller calendars for
  long-term monthly goals
  through the end of the second year

Teach us to number our days, that we may apply our hearts unto wisdom.

PSALM 90:12
(A PRAYER OF MOSES)

GOALS FOR TODAY
(a guide for daily planning in the first month)

Sunday

date

_____
_____
_____
_____
_____
_____
_____

Monday

date

_____
_____
_____
_____
_____
_____
_____

Tuesday

date

_____
_____
_____
_____
_____
_____
_____

Wednesday

date

Thursday

date

Friday

date

Saturday

date

GOALS FOR TODAY
(a guide for daily planning in the first month)

Sunday

date

_____
_____
_____
_____
_____
_____
_____
_____
_____

Monday

date

_____
_____
_____
_____
_____
_____
_____
_____
_____

Tuesday

date

_____
_____
_____
_____
_____
_____
_____
_____

Wednesday

date

Thursday

date

Friday

date

Saturday

date

GOALS FOR TODAY
(a guide for daily planning in the first month)

Sunday

date

_____
_____
_____
_____
_____
_____
_____
_____

Monday

date

_____
_____
_____
_____
_____
_____
_____
_____

Tuesday

date

_____
_____
_____
_____
_____
_____
_____

Wednesday

date

Thursday

date

Friday

date

Saturday

date

GOALS FOR TODAY
(a guide for daily planning in the first month)

Sunday

date

_____

Monday

date

_____

Tuesday

date

Wednesday

date

Thursday

date

Friday

date

Saturday

date

	Sunday	Monday	Tuesday
MONTH 1			

Wednesday	Thursday	Friday	Saturday

	Sunday	Monday	Tuesday
MONTH 2			

Wednesday	Thursday	Friday	Saturday

Sunday

Monday

Tuesday

MONTH 3

Wednesday	Thursday	Friday	Saturday

	Sunday	Monday	Tuesday
MONTH 4			

Wednesday	Thursday	Friday	Saturday

Sunday	Monday	Tuesday

MONTH 5

Wednesday	Thursday	Friday	Saturday

	Sunday	Monday	Tuesday

MONTH 6

Wednesday	Thursday	Friday	Saturday

Long-term monthly goals

Month 7

Month 8

Month 9

Month 10

Long-term monthly goals

_____

_____   *Month 11*

_____

_____

_____

_____

_____

_____

_____

_____

_____   *Month 12*

_____

_____

_____

_____

_____

_____

_____

_____

_____   *Month 13*

_____

_____

_____

_____

_____

_____

_____

_____   *Month 14*

_____

_____

_____

_____

_____

_____

Long-term monthly goals

Month 15

_____
_____
_____
_____
_____
_____
_____
_____

Month 16

_____
_____
_____
_____
_____
_____
_____
_____

Month 17

_____
_____
_____
_____
_____
_____
_____
_____

Month 18

_____
_____
_____
_____
_____
_____
_____
_____

Long-term monthly goals

Month 19

Month 20

Month 21

Month 22

Long-term monthly goals

Month 23

_____
_____
_____
_____
_____
_____
_____
_____

Month 24

_____
_____
_____
_____
_____
_____
_____
_____

HELP AND HOPE

8

Finding Supportive Relationships

If Ever Two Were Friends

If ever two were friends, then we:
One soul that dwells inside both you and me;
Two hearts entwined in trust and unity;
A freedom of expression wild and sweet;
A loyalty and bond death cannot sever;
An open love that can but last forever;
A singleness of mind so rarely seen,
As Jonathan and David's must have been;
Eyes that meet in silent understanding;
Forgiveness that replaces reprimanding;
Comfort shared through days of tribulation;
Harmony in songs of jubilation.
Our friendship is a joy beyond compare —
A precious gem: exquisite, rich and rare.

MARY HOLLINGSWORTH
AMERICAN POETRY ANTHOLOGY

KNOWING WHERE TO TURN for the right answers is not an easy task for a griever. Your questions can range from where to get emotional help to how to solve basic daily living problems. Such questions are perfectly normal.

Help *is* available if you know where to look — and, in some instances, if you meet certain qualifications. For some, though, the answers will come by building your own support network.

This section is designed to help you locate organizations that can help you. This list is not exhaustive. Some agencies will be available in your area and some will not, but most human services agencies have a referral service that can supply complete information for you in your area.

Self-help clearing-houses

NO MATTER in what area you feel you most need assistance, there's almost certainly a support group for you. The best way to find out if there's a chapter in your area (and when and where the group meets) is to call your local self-help clearinghouse. Volunteers at these numbers will put you in touch with the right support groups, and the service is free. Call the clearinghouse below nearest you.

California Self-Help Center
405 Hilgard Avenue
Los Angeles, California 90024
(213) 825-1799

Illinois Self-Help Center
1600 Dodge Avenue, Suite S-122
Evanston, Illinois 60201
(312) 328-0470

Massachusetts Clearinghouse
  of Mutual Help Groups
113 Skinner Hall
University of Massachusetts
Amherst, Massachusetts 01003
(413) 545-2313

Minnesota Mutual Help
  Resource Center
919 Lafond Avenue
St. Paul, Minnesota 55104
(612) 642-4060

Self-Help Clearinghouse
  of Greater Washington
100 N. Washington Street
Falls Church, Virginia 22046
(703) 536-4100

National Self-Help Clearinghouse
33 West 42nd Street
New York, New York 10036
(212) 642-2944

THE FOLLOWING national organizations can direct you to local support/help groups, and even provide helpful printed materials. Since individuals react to a loss in many different ways, we have listed support groups in different areas in which you, or a family member, may have need.

Alcoholics Anonymous
P.O. Box 459
Grand Central Station
New York, New York 10163
212-686-1100

Al-Anon/Alateen Family Group
   Headquarters
P.O. Box 182
Madison Square Station
New York, New York 10159
800-344-2666
212-302-7240

Center for Loss & Life Transition
3735 Broken Bow Road
Fort Collins, Colorado 80526
303-226-6050

The Compassionate Friends
P.O. Box 3696
Oak Brook, Illinois 60522
708-990-0010

Debtors Anonymous
314 W. 53rd Street
New York, New York 10019
212-969-0710

Emotions Anonymous
P.O. Box 4245
Saint Paul, Minnesota 55104
612-647-9712

Gamblers Anonymous
P.O. Box 17173
Los Angeles, California 90017
213-386-8789

Incest Survivors Anonymous
P.O. Box 5613
Long Beach, California 90800

The International Theos
   Foundation
717 Liberty Avenue
Pittsburgh, Pennsylvania 15222
412-471-7779

National Association for Children
   of Alcoholics
31582 Coast Highway, Suite B
South Laguna, California 92677
714-499-3889

The National Foundation for
   Sudden Infant Death, Inc.
8200 Professional Place, Suite 104
Landover, Maryland 20785
800-221-SIDS

Overcomers Outreach
2290 West Whittier Boulevard
La Habra, California 90631
213-697-3994

Overeaters Anonymous World
   Service Office
2190 190th Street
Torrance, California 90504
213-542-8363

The Widowed Persons Service
American Association of Retired
   Persons
3200 East Carson Street
Lakewood, California 90712

General help resources

THE LIST BELOW of agencies, services, and programs is a guide for identifying and locating general resources in your area. These agencies and groups can provide information and help with emotional and daily living concerns. (Additional services may also be available in your area, while some of those listed here may not be.)

CHURCHES
- grief support group
- special help or the bereaved
- caring community of faith

FUNERAL HOMES
- grief support
- assistance in obtaining survivor's benefits

SOCIAL SERVICE AGENCIES
- grief support
- assistance with daily living needs, such as food, housing, finances
- counseling
- information and referral
- day care for the elderly

MENTAL HEALTH AGENCIES
- grief counseling
- information and referral

COUNTY AND CITY PUBLIC HEALTH NURSING, AND VISITING NURSES ASSOCIATION
- home health care
- information and referral
- grief counseling

HOMEMAKERS UPJOHN
- home, health, and homemakers care

VETERANS SERVICES OFFICES
- funeral and burial expense assistance
- survivor benefits assistance

FAMILY SERVICES
- counseling

YELLOW PAGES
- phone numbers, addresses, and basic information

INFORMATION AND REFERRAL SERVICES
- comprehensive and current information about services and programs available in the community

MINISTERIAL COUNSELING SERVICES
- counseling
- grief support
- information and referral

SOCIAL SECURITY ADMINISTRATION
- funeral expense assistance
- survivor benefits assistance

CRISIS INTERVENTION
- information and referral
- grief counseling
- telephone reassurance

LEGAL SERVICES
- public legal service assistance for low income persons

AMERICAN RED CROSS
- information about services and programs available in the community

JOB SERVICE
- help with learning skills and locating employment

EDUCATIONAL INSTITUTIONS
- courses, seminars, and programs dealing with death and grief

HOSPITALS
- medical assistance
- counseling
- information and referral

SUPPORT is the most important asset the griever has. But too many people who have lost someone feel that support is *not* needed. They don't want to be a burden so they don't ask for support, or they don't know where to turn to find it. Unfortunately, for most, support is readily available but goes untapped.

Support may come in many forms — a person, an organization, or even a family network. The important thing to know is this: The responsibility for tapping and organizing your own support network is yours.

START WITH YOURSELF — using tools such as these:

- *Journaling* — Your Journal is your way of identifying feelings so you can properly respond to them. Use your Journal often, or you'll miss a valuable adjustment tool.

- *Balanced Lifestyle* — Exercise, eat well-balanced meals, get plenty of rest, do something fun just for you, relax. All these are important, though they may not seem important now. If healing is to come, you'll need to take care of yourself.

- *Education* — Ignorance hinders adjustment. Find out all you can about grief. Knowledge lessens fear, guilt, and complicated grief reactions. (Refer to the "Resource Bibliography" section at the end of this guide.)

Your support network

FAMILY AND FRIENDS — those who also share your loss — are a natural place to turn for support.

Society's rapid change makes our personal crises and losses more difficult by diminishing interpersonal and social support. So you may need to ask for help from family and friends by requesting one or more of these:

__encouragement cards   __physical help with tasks   __phone calls
__visits   __outings together   __their presence on significant days
__financial help   __legal help executing the will

Be fully aware that your family may "malfunction" when a death occurs. The whole family be thrown out of balance by the death of your loved one, just as you are. The deceased filled certain family roles which now must be filled by someone else. Such role replacement takes time.

Meanwhile you may experience friction and frustration among family members because they, like you, are in pain, and they don't know how to "fix" it. Be patient. Time will help sort out the problems.

Families are more apt to respond to your need for support if they are alerted to your need. Don't assume they know your needs; you must communicate them. You also may need to educate your family about grief and its phases. Purchase meaningful books for them, or share yours with them. The more they know about your grief, the better able to help you they will be.

Also, don't forget the children in your family who are grieving. (See Section 9, "Big Hurts for Little People.")

A caution: Remember that being your family member or friend does not mean a person is necessarily qualified to help and support you in the ways you need. Even with the best of intentions, a dear friend can hurt you by saying or doing the wrong things. You may need to tell those close to you that what you need most is a loving listener. Talk to them about this. Help them help you.

AN EXISTING SUPPORT NETWORK — made up of those who specialize in the field of caring — is the next level of help. Many people in this area are professionals, but not all. Often a lay person can provide care that is as good as or even better than the assistance you receive from those who make their living by counseling or facilitating support. The point to remember is to tap into the support *that feels right to you,* whether it's professional or not.

IF YOU CANNOT FIND an existing support network that is comfortable for you, you may want to begin your own group.

GOALS — Here are goals you may want to adopt in establishing an effective support group:

1. Better enable people to handle their own problems by taking constructive action.
2. Provide a safe atmosphere for every participant to feel free to communicate feelings — both positive and negative.
3. Help participants achieve a trusting relationship with others who have experienced a loss.
4. Help participants in problem management (dividing a larger problem into its smaller, more manageable parts).
5. Help participants develop and implement a personal growth action plan.
6. Supply lists of support agencies and organizations for individuals needing specialized help.

PURPOSE — Here's a suggested overall purpose statement for a loss support group:

"To help people who have experienced a loss to deal constructively with feelings and practical problems which result; and to help each other by sharing in the small-group experience."

TIME FRAME — We suggest that your group have stated starting and ending dates (the preferable time span from beginning to end is about six to ten weeks). More people will participate if they know in advance the duration of their commitment to the group.

GROUP SIZE — The most effective size for a loss adjustment group is from ten to fifteen persons.

FREQUENCY AND DURATION OF MEETINGS — Members usually expect the group's leader to guide them in discussing and deciding the frequency and duration of meetings. They may even prefer that the leader decide. Some people will enjoy weekly meetings, while others may prefer meeting less often. Sessions generally last from one and a half to two hours.

STRUCTURE — As the group begins, it's best to...
- choose a permanent location for the entire series.
- have all members agree to attend all meetings, and to not leave the group without announcing to the others his intention to do so.
- start and stop all meetings at the agreed-upon time.
- be in complete agreement about whether to allow new members to join the group after it's already underway, and about which topics should be discussed and which should be avoided.

SUBJECTS TO COVER — To help group members move forward in the adjustment process, here are topics that probably need to be addressed:
- Aloneness vs. Loneliness: How to Keep a Positive Attitude
- How Time Can Heal Great Wounds
- How Death of a Loved One Affects Your Self-Esteem
- How Your Family May React After the Death of a Loved One
- The Dynamics of Grief — How Does Grief Work?
- Will I Ever Be Happy Again?
- The Freedoms of Being Single
- Dealing with Guilt

SUPPORT GROUP RESOURCES —

For the leader/facilitator:

Clinebell, H. J., *Growth Groups* (Nashville: Abingdon Press, 1977). Gives the principles of setting up and leading growth groups, including grief groups.

Leslie, Robert, *Sharing Groups in the Church* (Nashville: Abingdon Press, 1971). Describes different types of sharing groups and how to lead them.

For *all* group members:

Caine, Lynne, *Widow* (New York: William Morrow and Company, 1974).

Clinebell, H. J., Jr., "A Grief Recovery Group" (Course 2B) and "The Crisis of Divorce-Growth Opportunities" (Course 3B), *Growth*

Counseling — Coping Constructively with Crisis (Nashville: Abingdon Press, 1974). A do-it- yourself set of courses on grief groups and divorce groups.

Clinebell, Howard, *Growth Counseling: Hope-Centered Methods of Actualizing Human Wholeness* (Nashville: Abingdon Press, 1979).

Curry, Cathleen L., *When Your Spouse Dies* (Notre Dame, Indiana: Ave Maria Press, 1990). A concise and practical source of help and advice on grief.

D'Arcy, Paula, *When Your Friend Is Grieving* (Wheaton, Illinois: Harold Shaw Publishers, 1990). A true story of growing through grief and how friends can help in practical, everyday ways.

Harris, Jerry; Sprang, Ginny; Komsak, Karen; *This Could Never Happen to Me* (Fort Worth, Texas: Mental Health Association of Tarrant County, 1987). A handbook for families of murder victims and people who assist their families.

Hickman, Martha Whitmore, *I Will Not Leave You Desolate* (Nashville: The Upper Room, 1982). Help for grieving parents.

Hollingsworth, Mary, *Rainbows* (Norwalk, Connecticut: The C. R. Gibson Company, 1989). A fully illustrated gift book to help people maintain their trust through troubled times.

Hollingsworth, Mary, *It's a One-derful Life!* (Fort Worth, Texas: Brownlow Publishing Company, 1988). A boxed gift book to present to people who are newly single again.

Jackson, Edgar, *You and Your Grief* (Manhasset, New York: Channel Press, 1961). A guide to the process of recovering from grief.

Kubler-Ross, Elizabeth, *On Death and Dying* (New York: The Macmillan Company, 1969). A paperback book for use in growth groups dealing with the subject of grief and dying.

Lewis, C. S., *A Grief Observed* (New York: Seabury Press, 1961). Lewis's moving account of his response to the death of his wife.

Oates, Wayne E., *Pastoral Care and Counseling in Grief and Separation* (Philadelphia: Fortress Press, 1976). Resources for helping the bereaved.

Stone, Howard, *Crisis Counseling* (Philadelphia: Fortress Press, 1976). An introduction to the theory and practice of crisis counseling.

Westberg, Granger, *Good Grief* (Rock Island, Illinois: Augustana, 1962). A paperback summarizing the insights about coping with the stages of recovery from grief. Can be used as a resource in a grief group.

BIG HURTS FOR LITTLE PEOPLE

9

Helping Children with Grief

The Psalmist said: "Even though I walk through the valley of the shadow of death...." The key words are walk through. You cannot remain in perpetual grief. Death, the "loss of innocence," can either lead you to the edge of the abyss and threaten your existence with meaninglessness and futility, or help you start to build the bridge that spans the chasm with those things of life that still count: memories, family, friendship, love.

Whatever your concept of a hereafter, strive to find purpose in the here, in this world. When you have sorted out your own feelings, you will be better able to understand your mourning children who come to you laden with questions and beset with fears. The real challenge is not just how to explain death to your children, but how to make peace with it yourself.

EARL GROLLMAN

GRIEF IS RARELY an individual experience. Rather, it's generally a family affair. Most families include both adults and children, so there may very well be children related to the deceased who also need help adjusting to the loss you all have suffered.

Unfortunately, children are often the forgotten ones. It's not that people don't care; the opposite is true. But many people feel uncomfortable talking to a child about death. They don't know how to start or what to say. Meanwhile, the child is left in pain with no tools to relieve the pain.

This section of the Guide will give you some practical pointers on how to help children adjust to their grief at the same time you are grieving.

167

A checklist for bereaved parents

FOLLOWING is a checklist of things to do for your grieving children, especially if the loss was your spouse and their parent, or perhaps your parent and their grandparent, or even your child and his or her sibling.

__ 1. Be mindful that it's difficult to distinguish between your own grief feelings and those of your children.

__ 2. Include your young people in what's going on — funeral arrangements, settling the estate, planning for the future. After all, it's their future, too.

__ 3. Tell them the factual truth, rather than assume they cannot handle it. Children are much better equipped to handle truth than we think.

__ 4. Know that you are a role model. Your children will tend to imitate your style of grief adjustment (such as either hoarding or sharing grief). They will tend to heal as you heal.

__ 5. Accept and grant permission to cry and to talk about what's happening. It's healthy, both for you and for them.

__ 6. Don't be surprised at the volatile emotions your child may show during his grief adjustment — anger one moment, depression the next. It's normal. Allow him to express his emotions, as long as they don't become destructive.

__ 7. Seek to *listen* as never before, without judging.

__ 8. Acknowledge and respond with reassurance to a young person's fear that you, too, might die and leave them. Tell them what practical arrangements have been made "just in case."

Being sensitive and sympathetic

IT'S IMPORTANT to be both sensitive to a child's needs at this time and to be sympathetic to his pain, which is likely a bit different from yours. Grief is unique to each person, and that's true of children, too. Here are suggestions to help you help them.

• Use the experience of other losses to help the child's understanding of what's happening now.
  —Talk about the death of a pet.
  —Point out examples of shared suffering, sympathy.
  —Avoid the "mistake" of quick replacement to ease pain.

- Be patient and seek to understand the child's reactions.
    - —Disbelief and self-defense might explain why a child appears casual or unaffected.
    - —Resist burdening a child with expectations of specific feelings or expressions of grief.
    - —Allow tears, anger, sadness.
    - —Be available, but not intrusive, respecting the child's privacy and personality.
- Maintain normalcy, as far as possible.
    - —Familiar routines and observances can provide a much needed stability.
    - —Provide reassurances about the future — finances, home, school, relatives, and so forth.
    - —Assure the child that smiles will eventually succeed tears, and that sorrow need not banish all good feelings.
    - —Communicate your own hopefulness to the child.
- Be truthful and direct.
    - —Be frank about the facts.
    - —Avoid euphemisms and figures of speech which might confuse the child and distort reality.
    - —Encourage questions and respond to them in ways that you really mean, ways that won't require retraction later.
- Refrain from overloading the child with responsibilities.
- Be alert to their fears: of sleep, of sickness, of their other parent's death.
- Include the child in the funeral activities, according to the child's maturity and level of interest, explaining in advance what will take place.
- Share and reinforce positive memories of the one who died.
    - —Remind the child of the love, concern, pride and joy that characterized the relationship.
    - —Give the child a possession or picture of the deceased as a keepsake.
- Accept the help and comfort the child offers you.

ADAPTED FROM "HOW TO HELP A BEREAVED CHILD"
BY MILDRED TENGBORN, IN *THE LUTHERAN STANDARD*

Helping hints by age level

CHILDREN REACT DIFFERENTLY to loss as they grow and mature. You cannot expect the same level of understanding from a preschooler as you do from a teenager. You need to recognize your child's ability to cope based on his or her age. Here is some information about child development that can enable you to help children at any age level adjust to loss. Put a check mark by the traits you have noticed in your own child so far.

Preschoolers
__ They cannot grasp the inevitability and finality of death.

__ They may grow to fear sleep or to overreact to illness if adults equate death with sleep ("Grandpa's gone to sleep") or with sickness.

__ They have short attention spans. (Responses to their questions, therefore, ought to be brief and repetitive.)

Six- and seven-year-olds
__ They do not yet believe they may someday die, but they are beginning to think their parents might.

__ They need help in learning how to talk about death. Using pictures or asking them to describe what's occurring might enable them to express their grief.

__ They sometimes worry about how the dead can eat, breathe, and so forth in the grave. They need explanations that adults consider obvious. For example, they need to be told that after death the body does not move, eyes do not see, ears do not hear, and so on.

__ They do not always ask for the specific answer they need. Try to determine just *what* they want to know before responding. If a child asks, "What makes people die?" you might reply by asking, "What do you think happened to Grandpa?"

Seven-to-nine-year-olds
__ They have begun to suspect that they themselves will die someday.

__ They have an active fantasy life and often seem curious about what happens to the body after death.

__ They often have difficulty expressing themselves. (Drawing pictures often provides an outlet for expressing their feelings. Say,

"Jenny, can you draw me a picture of how you feel?")
___ Peer and social pressures often inhibit their expression of emotions. (Allow them to cry, especially boys who are taught that "big boys don't cry.")

Ten-to twelve-year-olds
___ They are not old enough to shoulder head-of-household responsibility. (Spare them from thinking of themselves as "the man of the house" or "the mother of the family.")
___ They are developing a heightened interest in life's spiritual aspects. Introducing or reaffirming the family's faith and religious values can prove supportive.
___ They desire information about death, but may not know how to ask for it. Books, read separately or together and then discussed, might enhance understanding and adjustment.

Teenagers
___ Even at this age, talking about loss can be difficult. (To stimulate useful exchanges, ask questions such as these: *How old is old? How old would you like to be before you die? What accomplishments would you like to be remembered for when you die?*)
___ The frequency of suicide in this age group is high. (This underscores the importance of hearing and sharing opinions on the causes of despair, the reasons for hope, and the meaning of life.)

SUGGESTIONS BY BARBARA COYNE, PH.D.

"My Memory Book"

JUST AS YOU have been encouraged to record your memories of the deceased, you can help your child record his precious memories of the deceased. Here's how:

1. Buy a small scrapbook for your child to use as "My Memory Book of [the deceased person's name]."
2. Let the child write the title of the book on the first page.
3. Talk to the child about what things he wants to put in his memory book. Help the child make a list of them — photos, stories about fun times, brochures from family vacations, souvenirs from outings, napkins or matchbook covers from favorite restaurants, and so on.

4. Help the child gather up the items he wants to include in the memory book.
5. Tell the child that he can work on his memory book *when he wants to.* Don't force him to work on it unless he's ready. It's not important that the book be finished immediately...or ever. He may wish to continue adding things to the book as time goes along.
6. Let the child put things in the memory book the way *he* wants them, not you. It's his book. Don't help him unless he asks you to.
7. If the child is too young to write, help him write down stories about favorite adventures or family times. Let him paste in pictures from old magazines that remind him of the story.
8. Let him cry as he works on the book if he needs to. It's healthy. Cry with him, if you need to.
9. Let the memory book be the child's private treasure. Don't read it or look at it unless he invites you to do so. If he knows no one else is going to look at the book, he will likely be more open with his grief, which will help him adjust to the loss.
10. Let the child choose a "place of honor" for the book to be kept.

Grandma's Swing

I love to sit in Grandma's swing
And hear the whispering snow;
Dangling feet
    and rhythmed squeak —
A front seat at the show.

Flakey bites of winter clouds
In crusty layers lie
With snow peaks topping
    rich brown soil
Like chocolate icebox pie.

And from her kitchen, luscious smells
Of cornbread sticks and greens,
Porkchops, squash,
    and all topped off
With scoops of snow ice cream.

Melancholy memories
Of snow and Grandma's swing
Drift in heaps upon my heart
Awaiting hopeful spring.

MARY HOLLINGSWORTH

LEGALLY SPEAKING

10

Legal Planning

THE LAW PLAYS a major part in adjusting to a significant loss through death. Legal matters must be handled now, though you may not be thinking clearly. Yet this is also a time when your clearest thinking is required to avoid making costly mistakes. During this complicated time, your attorney can be your best friend and most valuable resource.

Unless you are an attorney yourself, hiring a competent attorney is probably a good investment at this time. Legal matters are complicated and specialized. Acting as your own attorney may seem like a wise economic decision, but without proper legal training you run the risk of serious legal mistakes resulting in major financial losses.

NOTE: *This section includes only a brief description of some of the more general legal considerations involved with settling an estate. You should NOT use this book as a substitute for an attorney. The authors are not, and do not claim to be, attorneys. On the contrary, we advise you to seek the professional counsel of a licensed, practicing attorney, to whom we defer in all legal matters.*

Your attorney can assist by filing the deceased's will with the probate court, helping you apply for Social Security and insurance benefits (if appropriate), estimating income taxes and making sure you file them properly and in a timely way, and handling many other details that are easy to overlook during this crisis time.

Naturally, if you already have an attorney you know and trust, you'll want to take these matters to that person.

Record your choice of attorney here:

attorney's name: _____

firm's name: _____

address: _____

city/state/zip: _____

telephone number: _____

notes: _____

_____

How to select an attorney

THE MOST IMPORTANT factors in selecting an attorney are rapport and confidence. He needs to be someone with whom you can be comfortable and someone you can trust completely. Your attorney needs to be able to patiently communicate complex legal matters to you on your own level of understanding. This is important because your attorney does not make decisions *for* you (unless you ask him to). Instead, he presents you with the facts and your legal options; then you choose the option that best fits your situation and comfort level.

REFERRALS FROM FAMILY AND FRIENDS — The best way to select a competent attorney is to ask your friends, family, and business associates for references. If they have been pleased with an attorney's performance, personality, and professionalism, you may find that person is a good choice for you, too.

ORGANIZATIONS AND SERVICES —

The **American Bar Association** (ABA) will refer you to a local legal referral service that can advise you. The ABA answers calls from 9 A.M. to 5 P.M., Central Time.

> American Bar Association
> Lawyers Referral and Information Service
> 1155 East 60th Street
> Chicago, IL 60637
> (312) 332-1111

The **National Legal Aid and Defender Association** is a national clearinghouse of organizations that provide legal services for people who are unable to pay.

> National Legal Aid and Defender Association
> 1625 K Street, NW
> 8th Floor
> Washington, DC 20006
> (202) 452-0620 (9 A.M. to 5:30 P.M., Eastern Time)

The **National Resource Center for Consumers of Legal Services** helps people who need to choose an attorney or who need to complain about an attorney.

> National Resource Center for Consumers of Legal Services
> 3254 Jones Court, NW
> Washington, DC 20007
> (202) 338-0714 (weekdays, 9 A.M. to 5 P.M., Eastern Time)

You may also have reason to contact the U. S. government's legal offices:

> United States Department of Justice
> Tenth Street and Constitution Avenue, NW
> (202) 633-2000

If all else fails, your telephone book's *Yellow Pages* will reveal the names, phone numbers, addresses, and other pertinent information about various law firms and attorneys in your area.

ATTORNEYS AND THEIR SPECIALTIES — Keep in mind that attorneys specialize in particular areas of law practice. Some attorneys are corporate (business) attorneys. Some are tax attorneys. Some are bankruptcy specialists. And some specialize in "probate" law.

For your needs at this time, it is best to find a probate attorney who is abreast of recent changes, rules, and regulations dealing with this specialty area. His more current and thorough knowledge of probate procedures can save you large amounts of money.

It's true that almost any licensed attorney can "figure it out eventually," but the time and money expended will likely be much greater.

CHECK THEM OUT — When you have tentatively selected an attorney, set up an interview to get acquainted, and to find out specifically what your financial and legal arrangement with him or her will be. Discuss the scope of the legal service you need, and have the attorney describe the work necessary to accomplish your legal goals.

During the interview, evaluate for yourself these things:

- How comfortable are you with the attorney? If the attorney is a man and you're a woman, would you be more comfortable with a woman attorney? (Or vice versa?)
- Does the attorney have a sense of humor, if that's important to you?
- Are you confident that this attorney will maintain strict confidence about your personal affairs?
- Does this attorney look and sound professional?
- Does his office look organized and efficient?
- How does he interact with other people in his office?
- On a scale of one (lowest) to ten (highest), how would you rate your impression of this attorney? (Circle the number below that represents your feelings.)

1   2   3   4   5   6   7   8   9   10

Your attorney, the law, and you

WRITTEN LAW is a precise discipline that has been refined continually during the course of time. Attorneys, on the other hand, are human beings who can and do make mistakes in practicing that discipline. So it's important for you to monitor constantly the decisions and options your attorney recommends to you. Ultimately, *you* must be responsible for the legal decisions and actions you take. Your attorney is only your legal adviser.

Don't give your attorney absolute freedom to decide your legal affairs. Such an arrangement presents too many opportunities for misunderstanding, lack of control for you, and in some cases, unfortunately, even embezzlement of estate funds by an occasional unscrupulous attorney. Protect yourself and the deceased's estate by being involved in the legal matters that must be settled.

Also, be wary of any attorney who encourages you to step outside the law in any way. The risk of operating outside the law is always greater than the benefit. Remember that laws are made to protect right-living people and to punish wrong-living people. And be assured that the legal system works well in most instances. Tell your attorney that you do not want to take any legal risks, that you want to operate totally within the safe boundaries of the law.

Ask your attorney to provide you with photocopies of everything he does for you, including all court pleadings, certificates, questionnaires, and all correspondence and other paperwork, both incoming and outgoing. This will help you stay abreast of what's happening all the time, and you won't be surprised by decisions with which you do not agree. This also helps keep the attorney on his toes, ensuring the quality of his work; he knows you, who hold the purse strings, are reviewing it.

If you receive a copy of some document or piece of correspondence that you do not understand, call the law firm and have it explained to your satisfactory understanding. Don't leave yourself in the dark.

How to keep your legal fees down

IT'S EXPENSIVE to "rent" an attorney's time — there's no doubt about it. He's an expert, and experts are always high-priced. Therefore you may want to follow one or more of these suggestions to keep your attorney's fees to a minimum.

1. If you're dealing with a senior attorney in a law firm, ask him to let his paralegal or a junior attorney do most of the legwork and preparation of standard legal paperwork for his review. That way, rather than pay a senior attorney's hourly rate, you will pay the paralegal or junior attorney's rate for most of the routine services they provide. At the same time you have the benefit of the senior and more experienced attorney's review and approval.

2. Make your own photocopies whenever possible. Ask the attorney's secretary how many copies he will need of the various documents you are required to provide. Make those copies yourself to avoid the higher cost of having the firm make them.

3. Don't call your attorney just to visit. From the moment the attorney says hello until he says goodbye, his clock will be running and you'll be paying his hourly rate. If you must ask a question, keep it short. Better yet, first contact the junior attorney or paralegal with your question. Let him research the answer and get back to you.

4. Do as much telephone research as you possibly can for the

attorney. And if you can track down general information your-self, do so. You can decrease much of an attorney's time and telephone charges in these ways.

5. If you have any legal background or experience at all, you might wish to draft certain types of pleadings and documents yourself. A trip to a law library (to find one locally, check the *Yellow Pages*) can provide you with formats and sample word-ings for most types of documents. These are what your attorney himself will often follow. You can type the documents yourself and simply have your attorney review them for you. *Caution:* This is not a simple procedure. If you have no legal experience, it's probably best to let your attorney prepare the documents.

6. Recognize that legal negotiations are usually a matter of com-promise. Be prepared to give and take with other parties involved in some types of settlement procedures. If you refuse to compromise or give up anything, legal costs can skyrocket due to the added hours and services required of your attorney. "Standing your ground" in a legal suit can often be false economy; what you save in the estate may be eaten up by the legal fees required to save it.

Legal resources

THE BOOKS AND RESOURCES listed below can provide insight into the legalities involved with a loss through death. This list is not exhaustive, and a trip to a law library or public library can provide you with several other valuable references.

Everybody's Guide to the Law, Melvin Belli and Allen P. Wilkinson (Harcourt Brace Jovanovich, 1986).
Black's Law Dictionary, Henry C. Black, fifth edition (West, 1979).
When Your Spouse Dies, Cathleen L. Curry (Notre Dame, Indiana: Ave Maria Press, 1990).
A Family Guide to Estate Planning, Funeral Arrangements, and Settling an Estate After Death, Theodore E. Hughes and David Klein (New York: Charles Scribner's Sons, 1983).
Reader's Digest Family Legal Guide: A Complete Encyclopedia of Law for the Layman (Reader's Digest, 1981).
Handbook of Everyday Law, Martin J. Ross and Jeffrey Ross (Harper & Row, 1981).

PUT A CHECK MARK by each item below as you accomplish it. (Cross out those items that do not apply to you.) This will help you visualize the progress you are making in taking care of legal matters arising from your loss.

Your legal checklist

__ Retain an attorney to help settle the estate.

__ Order a dozen copies of the death certificate.

__ File the will for probate.

__ Notify all persons affected by the provisions of the will.

__ Make a complete list of all estate assets.

__ Make a complete list of all estate debts.

__ Settle all funeral expense accounts.

__ Change the designations on all banking accounts and negotiable paper held by the deceased, as appropriate.

__ Change the beneficiary designations on all documents where the deceased was previously listed.

__ File claims for benefits payable under the provisions of the deceased's insurance policies, Social Security, veteran's benefits, and other benefit plans and programs.

__ Change designations on all property titles (for automobiles, real estate, boats, and so on).

__ Change the telephone book listing for the next printing.

__ Notify your state's driver's license bureau.

__ Cancel or change designations on all credit cards and accounts held by the deceased.

__ Cancel or change designations on all subscriptions held by the deceased.

__ Terminate or change any partnership or business contracts held by the deceased, as appropriate.

__ Pay all outstanding debts of the estate, as appropriate.

__ Notify any sources of continuing income for the deceased's estate (such as royalties, dividends, and interest).

UNFINISHED BUSINESS

Settling the Estate

11

VIRTUALLY EVERYONE who dies, unless he is a minor or in abject poverty, leaves unfinished business that his survivors must complete. For a time there will be continuing income and expenses related to the deceased's estate. He may be entitled to a tax refund, final salary checks, monies from employee benefits programs, stock dividends, military retirement income, or income from the sale of property. Usually he has outstanding debts, such as household utility bills, car and house payments, and other accounts that must be settled.

In short, adjusting to the loss of your loved one also involves settling and closing his or her personal and financial matters. This section will give you guidelines about matters that need attention, as well as places to record pertinent information.

A WILL is an expression of a person's final wishes, primarily about the handling and distribution of his earthly possessions. Some people make a will and some don't. In either case, state laws provide a proper procedure for settling and closing a deceased person's estate. A person who dies after having made a will is said to have died "testate" (with a testament or will). A person who dies without having made a will is said to have died "intestate" (without a testament or will).

Naturally, if a will exists, the survivors must, by law, make every effort to see that the deceased's final wishes are carried out. If there is no will, then the state's "law of intestate succession" takes over and dictates how the deceased's property and possessions are to be distributed. The law of intestate succession exists to protect the

It is important that when we come to die we have nothing left to do but die.

CHARLES HODGE

The will, other legal papers, and the law

natural heirs to a person's estate. If the one you have lost had no will, contact your attorney to find out the particulars of your state's law of intestate succession.

POWER OF A WILL — Unfortunately there are common misconceptions about the power of a will that, if unknown, can render a person's wishes impossible to fulfill by the survivors. Remember this: A will is subject to law; law is not subject to a will.

A will cannot override the power of other legal papers. For instance, if the deceased has stated in his will that his house is to be bequeathed to his wife, but the title to that house is in joint ownership between the deceased and his son, the son will receive the house, not the wife. The will does not have power over the title to the house. *Remember:* It's vital that a person's legal papers reflect the same ultimate wishes that his or her will reflects. Only then can the will effectively carry out the deceased's final wishes.

Also, a will cannot override the general laws of the land. For instance, if a person's will instructs the executor of the will to perform some illegal act in settling the estate, that part of the will is considered by the court to be invalid and unenforceable.

In addition, a will cannot override your state's general probate laws. Some states have very strict probate laws to protect a person's surviving family members. For instance, the will might bequeath "everything" to the spouse, but the state's law may require that half of a person's estate be divided equally among his surviving children. In that case, the spouse will receive only half the estate. The will does not govern the law.

Responsibilities of the executor

WILLS TYPICALLY NAME an executor to settle the testator's estate according to the will. The executor is the deceased's chosen personal representative to ensure that his final wishes are carried out. The executor has a fiduciary responsibility to execute the will as carefully and exactly as possible. It is advisable to work closely with an attorney in order to legally and efficiently perform these duties.

Here are some of the responsibilities an executor must shoulder to settle and close a more complex estate. He must...

- collect all outstanding income to the estate.
- manage the current or ongoing estate.

- settle the final affairs of the estate according to the will but within the law.
- with an attorney's or the court's help, determine the validity of the will.
- identify and notify the beneficiaries named in the will.
- notify the deceased's creditors and determine the legitimacy of their claims against the estate.
- ensure that the remaining assets of the estate, after the debts have been paid, are properly distributed to the named beneficiaries or natural heirs.

DO I HAVE TO SERVE? — If you have been named the executor of the deceased's estate, but you don't feel up to the job, remember this: As the deceased's personal representative, you have the right to hire attorneys, accountants, and other professionals to help you work through the responsibilities and affairs of settling the estate. Besides that, you are generally entitled to be paid for your work on the estate and to be reimbursed for any expenses you incur, unless the will specifically states otherwise.

On the other hand, you can decline to serve as executor. Often a will designates an alternate executor. If not, the court will appoint someone else to serve, generally following this priority list:

1. The surviving spouse who is a named beneficiary in the will.
2. Anyone else who is named as a beneficiary of the will.
3. The surviving spouse of the deceased, when there is no will.
4. Another heir to the estate, when there is no will.
5. A creditor of the estate.
6. An attorney, a bank, or someone else appointed by the court as a last resort.

One thought to consider: Even if you're not professionally qualified to serve, your care for the deceased or your vested interest in the estate will likely help you do a more careful job of settling the estate than some disinterested party, such as a bank or lawyer.

If you *do* decide to serve, the first step is to have the attorney file the standard petition with the court to officially appoint you as the executor of the will.

Estate assets

THE FIRST RESPONSIBILITY in settling the estate is to compile a complete list of estate assets, both current and ongoing. Use the following chart to calculate the estate's total assets. Be sure to include amounts that are held by the deceased individually and jointly.

Cash and Liquid Assets

checking accounts _____

_____

savings accounts _____

_____

_____

cash value of
life insurance policies _____

_____

savings bonds _____
equity in pension funds _____

_____

money market funds _____

_____

brokerage funds _____

trusts _____

_____

debts owed to the estate _____

_____

_____

_____

_____

other cash and liquid assets _____

_____

_____

TOTAL Cash and Liquid Assets _____

Deceased's Personal Holdings

automobiles (current value) _____

_____

_____

home(s) _____

_____

boat(s) _____

_____

major appliances _____

_____

_____

_____

_____

furs and jewelry _____

_____

antiques and collectibles(total) _____

art (total) _____

other personal holdings _____

_____

_____

Total Personal Holdings _____

Estate Investments

common stocks _____

preferred stocks

corporate and municipal bonds _____

mutual funds _____

_____

certificates of deposit _____

_____

_____

_____

business investments _____

_____

_____

real estate investments _____

_____

_____

_____

_____

IRAs _____
other estate investments _____

_____

Total Estate Investments _____

(Cash and Liquid Assets
+ Personal Holdings
+ Estate Investments =)
TOTAL ESTATE ASSETS _____

Estate debts

The next step in settling the estate is to compile a complete list of outstanding debts owed by the estate. Use the following chart to list the liabilities of the estate.

Liabilities

household bills due _____

_____

medical bills due _____

_____

personal bills due _____

legal fees due _____

_____

revolving charge card debts _____

_____

_____

_____

bank card debts _____

_____

_____

other charge card debts _____

_____

federal estate taxes due _____
state taxes due _____
other taxes due _____

_____

outstanding mortgage _____
outstanding loans _____

_____

stock margin accounts payable _____
funeral expenses due _____

_____

other outstanding debts _____

_____

_____

_____

TOTAL ESTATE DEBTS _____

TO FIND the beginning net worth of the deceased's estate: *Subtract the*
Total Estate Debts *from the* ***Total Estate Assets*** in the space provided
below. Keep in mind, however, that ongoing expenses in settling the
estate will be incurred. For instance, there may be court costs, attorney
fees, executor's reimbursements, telephone and postage costs, and
other items required to close the affairs of the estate. There may be
ongoing income to the estate, such as royalties or dividends.

**Estate
net worth**

Total Estate Assets _____

— Total Estate Debts (_____)

= ESTATE NET WORTH _____

Personal items: Deciding who gets what

WHEN THE WILL specifies which relative or friend is to receive particular personal items from the estate, that makes it simple. When there is no list of "who gets what," matters can get complicated. The larger the number of heirs, the more complex the problem becomes.

How can you be fair? Who should go first? How can you maintain equality and impartiality? Here are some suggestions on ways to divide the deceased's personal items in fair and reasonable ways while maintaining your sanity, too.

CHILDREN ONLY — To avoid possible conflicts between in-laws, restrict involvement in the distribution process to children of the deceased only. Request all others to not be present while the distribution is decided. (An exception: the surviving spouse of a deceased child who is to receive equal shares to hold for the grandchildren.)

CATEGORIZE — Make a complete list of the deceased's personal belongings, dividing them into "Major Items" and "Minor Items." Large appliances, bigger pieces of furniture, and other expensive personal items (such as jewelry, clocks, works of art, antiques, collectibles, family heirlooms) will likely be major items. Clothing (except furs and other expensive articles), small pieces of furniture, smaller appliances, and other less expensive items will likely be minor items. This list will help you maintain financial equality.

ESTATE SALE — The least complicated way to ensure total financial equality in distribution is to hold an estate sale. When all personal items have been sold, income from the sale is simply divided equally among the proper recipients. However, this procedure eliminates the privilege of family members retaining sentimental items and family heirlooms.

INTER-FAMILY SALE — Estimate the total value of the personal items to be distributed. Then, let various members of the family purchase (from their share of estate wealth) the personal items they want from the other members.

FROM ELDEST TO YOUNGEST — One excellent way to distribute personal items is a hands-on process. Have everyone involved in the personal distribution meet at the site where the personal items are kept. Then, using the list of major and minor items, let the eldest child choose one of the major items he wishes to have. Then let the next eldest child choose, and so on down to the youngest child. After each child has chosen, start again with the eldest and repeat the procedure until all the major items the heirs wish to keep have been chosen. Repeat the entire procedure for the minor items.

Any unwanted items left over can be put into a limited estate sale, with proceeds divided equally among the recipients.

A variation of this procedure is to provide numbers to be drawn by each heir. After everyone draws a number, turns are taken in number order instead of from eldest child to youngest. This procedure is especially appropriate if someone besides a child of the deceased is entitled to an equal share along with the children.

DIVIDE AND CHOOSE — Another way to promote fairness is to let one of the heirs divide the personal items into equal shares, making lists of the items in each share. All the *other* heirs then choose (either by drawing numbers, or from eldest to youngest) which share they want. The last remaining share goes to the one who divided the items in the beginning.

"TAKE-BACK" — Another distribution procedure is to begin by allowing each heir to "take back" any personal items that he or she gave to the deceased through the years. The remaining items can be distributed by using one of the methods described above.

APPRAISALS — It may be necessary or advisable to obtain professional appraisals of valuable items such as jewelry, furs, works of art, antiques, and collectibles. This helps ensure that a fair price is received for them if they are sold, or that equality can be maintained if they are divided among the heirs. Appraisals should be obtained in writing for all to see. You may be required to pay an appraisal fee, which should be deducted from the assets of the estate.

Special considerations

ALMOST EVERY FAMILY has special situations to consider when settling the estate of a loved one — such as minor children who must be protected in the distribution, a handicapped person to be consulted or protected, or elderly parents of the deceased who need special care that the deceased had once provided. Your attorney can advise you in the best ways and ethics of handling these special considerations.

TIME OUT FOR ME

Your Personal Checkup

12

FOR WEEKS NOW, perhaps even months, you have been struggling through your grief while trying to handle the personal affairs of the one you've lost. Obviously those responsibilities have been urgent and necessary.

Meanwhile, have you been overlooking your own needs? If so, you're certainly not alone. It's perfectly normal for grievers to concentrate for a time on the one they have lost rather than themselves — in fact it's practically unavoidable, considering the myriad of details that must be sorted out and settled.

Now that the initial pressure has passed, though, it's time to spend a little time thinking about your own health and continued happiness. After all, your body and mind have been through a lot recently. It's not unusual for grievers to experience physical distress or illness in some form during the months of intense grief. And that can't be ignored for too long.

This section gives you a place to do some personal planning. It's a place to record your medical and dental history and current status, plus other pertinent personal data. Once recorded here, that information will help you know what steps may need to be taken to restore or enhance your personal health and happiness.

Below are things you should do for yourself to help increase your peace of mind. Put a check mark by each step as you accomplish it, so you can see your continued progress toward loss adjustment and a return to a full life:

___ Make an appointment for a medical checkup.
___ Make an appointment for a dental checkup.

___ Make an appointment for an eye examination.
___ Make an appointment with your attorney to revise your own will and other personal papers.
___ Make an appointment with your financial adviser to discuss your personal finances, and to plan for your future financial security.
___ If you've decided to go back to school, make an appointment with a student adviser at the school to discuss the courses and direction you wish to take.
___ If you want to take up a new hobby, make an appointment with a teacher to gather information and get started.
___ *Other:* _____

_____

Medical record

doctor's name: _____
doctor's specialty: _____
address: _____
city/state/zip: _____
telephone number: _____

doctor's name: _____
doctor's specialty: _____
address: _____
city/state/zip: _____
telephone number: _____

doctor's name: _____
doctor's specialty: _____
address: _____
city/state/zip: _____
telephone number: _____

doctor's name: _____
doctor's specialty: _____
address: _____
city/state/zip: _____
telephone number: _____

date of your last physical exam: _____

doctor who examined you: _____

results: _____

age: _____   height: _____   weight: _____

blood type: _____ Rh: _____

pulse rate: _____   blood pressure: _____/_____

vision: _____left _____right   hearing: _____left _____right

Have you ever had...

(*Put a check mark by any of these you have experienced*)

__allergies   __kidney trouble   __anemia   __measles   __arthritis
__menstrual cramps   __asthma   __migraine headaches
__chicken pox   __mononucleosis   __concussion   __mumps
__diabetes   __pneumonia   __eczema   __polio   __epilepsy
__emotional problems   __rheumatic fever   __severe sinus trouble
__frequent fainting   __chronic sore throats   __heart murmur
__tuberculosis   __hepatitis   __whooping cough   __hernia
__hives   __other: _____

_____

hospitalizations/surgeries —

dates: *hospital:*   *reason:*

_____

_____

_____

_____

_____

_____

_____

medications you are now taking —

name: *dosage/frequency:*   *for:*

_____

_____

_____

_____

_____

_____

_____

Describe any current medical treatment you are receiving:

_____
_____
_____
_____

other important medical information:

_____
_____
_____
_____

Have you experienced any type of physical distress or change since your last physical exam? *yes*___ *no*___ If so, describe: _____

_____
_____

Dental record

dentist's name: _____
address: _____
city/state/zip: _____
telephone number: _____

date of last dental exam: _____
type of work performed: _____
Have you experienced any dental pain or changes since your last dental exam? *yes*___ *no*___
If so, describe: _____
_____

Are you allergic to any dental anesthetics? *yes*___ *no*___
If so, which one(s): _____
Have you ever had any dental surgery? *yes*___ *no*___
If so, describe: _____
_____

other important dental information: _____
_____

ophthalmologist/optometrist: _____

address: _____

city/state/zip: _____

telephone number: _____

date of last eye exam: _____

results: ___normal __glasses __contacts

Have you experienced any change in your visual ability since your last eye exam? *yes___ no___*

If so, describe: _____

_____

_____

Do you currently have any type of eye disease or abnormality?

yes___ no___ If so, describe: _____

_____

_____

Have you ever had eye surgery? *yes___ no___*

If so, describe: _____

_____

Eye care record

health insurance company: _____

agent's name: _____

claims address: _____

city/state/zip: _____

agent's telephone number: _____

claims telephone number: _____

plan or policy number: _____ I.D. number: _____

_____

Medicare I.D. number: _____

Medicaid I.D. number: _____

_____

supplemental policy company: _____

agent's name: _____

claims address: _____

city/state/zip: _____

agent's telephone number: _____

claims telephone number: _____

plan or policy number: _____ I.D. number: _____

Insurance information

dental insurance company: _____
agent's name: _____
claims address: _____
city/state/zip: _____
agent's telephone number: _____
claims telephone number: _____
plan or policy number: _____ I.D. number: _____

_____

eye care insurance company: _____
agent's name: _____
claims address: _____
city/state/zip: _____
agent's telephone number: _____
claims telephone number: _____
plan or policy number: _____ I.D. number: _____

_____

FEELING FINE

Emotional Planning

13

> *When the hurts of today have drained our endurance, and we are crushed and broken by despair, when we feel ourselves frozen in an emotional paralysis that numbs our senses so that nothing works, our arms and legs hang limp and even our eyes slump back into our heads, we grope for the edge of tomorrow. Its promise of a new beginning is only a day away, and its resource is hope. When we think that we have nothing left, we need to remember we still have hope.*
>
> FAY ANGUS
> *RUNNING AROUND IN SPIRITUAL CIRCLES*

YOUR EMOTIONS may be the aspect of your loss adjustment that seems most out of control for the longest period of time. Emotions are volatile; you're in the pits one moment, and on top of the world the next. You may cry uncontrollably or even laugh uncontrollably. You'll be depressed, worried, nervous, afraid, relieved, guilty, and happy, almost all at the same time. You wonder, *Won't these emotions ever settle down?*

Yes, they will…eventually. In the meantime, it's advisable to seek help. Rather than merely reacting to the emotional eruptions as they come, find someone who can help you plan you emotional future.

He who conceals his grief finds no remedy for it.

OLD TURKISH PROVERB

How to select a counselor or support group

CHOOSING A PERSON or method to support you during your intense grief-adjustment period can be intimidating. That's especially true when grief is unfamiliar to you. Who should you choose? And on what basis? This section offers you general guidelines for decision-making in this area.

First, there is more than one "right" answer about the kind of support that fits the needs of those who are adjusting to loss. Some grievers like the dynamics of a group experience where they can learn from others' input, but others won't be comfortable opening up in the presence of more than one other person. Use your feelings in this process. If a group structure feels comfortable, it's probably right for you. If it doesn't, perhaps a personal counselor in a one-on-one setting is a better choice.

Second, don't be afraid to ask questions during the selection process. If a counselor is offended by your questions about his or her credentials, successes, and referrals by former clients, find one who isn't.

Third, make sure the counselor specializes in your area of loss adjustment. Just because a person offers therapy or counseling does not mean he is knowledgeable about the kind of grief you are experiencing. To find out, simply ask.

Here are some specialized areas of counseling:

- loss of a child
- homicide loss
- natural disaster loss
- cancer loss
- suicide loss
- military-related loss
- loss by natural causes

Fourth, choose a counselor or support group by asking for referrals from your friends and family. Those who personally have gone through counseling or group therapy will likely be the most help to you. You can also ask other professionals — such as doctors, social workers or psychologists — for referrals. Keep asking several sources until you find a name or names surfacing often. Having confidence in the program or professional you choose will go a long way toward healthy adjustment.

Fifth, analyze the goals of the counselor or group. The overall goal of grief counseling should be to help the survivor complete any unfinished business with the deceased and to be able to say a final goodbye. This approach will include these secondary goals:

1. To increase belief in the reality of the loss.
2. To help in dealing with both the expressed and latent effects of the loss.
3. To help in overcoming various obstacles to readjustment after the loss.
4. To encourage a healthy emotional withdrawal from the deceased, and a comfortable reinvestment of that emotion in another relationship or endeavor.

Sixth, choose a counselor or support group by method. You may choose from among three options:

1. Professional services by trained doctors, nurses, psychologists, or social workers.
2. Volunteer services with professional support. (These programs are usually connected to a hospital support system or to a church counseling center.)
3. Self-help support groups, whether facilitated by chaplains or trained lay volunteers.

What about medication?

THE USE OF MEDICATION for managing acute but normal grief has been much discussed. The general feeling among professionals is that medication should be used sparingly and always under the care of a doctor. These medications should be used to provide relief from anxiety or insomnia, rather than for depression.

It is usually *not* advisable to take antidepressant medications while in acute grief. Antidepressants take a long time to work, rarely relieve normal grief symptoms, and could pave the way for an abnormal grief response. Drugs are unnecessary in most cases.

> *Blessed are those whose dreams are shaped by their hopes...*
> *not by their hurts!*
>
> ROBERT SCHULLER *THE BE(HAPPY) ATTITUDES*

When should I begin grief counseling?

GRIEF COUNSELING usually can begin a week or so after the funeral, at the earliest. In the days immediately after the loss the bereaved person often is still in a state of numbness or shock, and is not yet ready to come to grips with his confusion. This is often too soon for tbe person to readily benefit from counseling, unless there has been contact with the counselor prior to the loss. (In situations where there is an awareness of impending death, family members may contact a counselor for preparatory counseling. After the loss, they may desire additional contact with the counselor.)

Here again there is no set rule, and this guideline should not be followed too rigidly. When to begin counseling depends entirely on the individual, the setting of the death, and surrounding circumstances.

Helping your counselor help you

Your counselor generally will first want to assess where you are emotionally. He will determine the significance of your loss, noting your responses to the loss experience as you talk with him. You can help the process along by having your thoughts organized as much as possible. Complete the following information, and take it with you to your first session with the counselor/support group.

History of Losses

List any other significant losses you may have experienced in your life.

person lost: _____
relationship to you: _____
date of loss: _____
Why was the loss significant? _____
_____
_____

person lost: _____
relationship to you: _____
date of loss: _____
Why was the loss significant? _____
_____
_____

person lost: _____

relationship to you: _____

date of loss: _____

Why was the loss significant? _____

_____

_____

person lost: _____

relationship to you: _____

date of loss: _____

Why was the loss significant? _____

_____

What seems to be your personal pattern for handling loss experiences?

_____

_____

_____

_____

_____

Outline the sequence of events leading up to the death, surrounding the death, and immediately following the death of your recently lost loved one. Note any unusual or unique occurrences that may be of interest.

_____

_____

_____

_____

_____

_____

_____

_____

_____

_____

_____

_____

Identify any fears, guilt feelings, anger, or confusion associated with your loss. (Refer to Section 5, "A Time to Refocus," where you may already have worked through some of these things on your own.) Remember: The more open you are with your counselor, the better he will be able to help you.

_____
_____
_____
_____
_____
_____
_____
_____
_____
_____

As you write in your Grief Adjustment Journal, remember to look back from time to time, noting progress in adjustment, lessons learned, and strengths gained since suffering your loss. For your counselor's benefit, you may want to list some of these steps of progress below.

_____
_____
_____
_____
_____
_____
_____
_____
_____
_____

For the bereaved, storytelling may mean revisiting again and again the site of the death or going to the cemetery frequently. The effect will be the same. The storytelling eases the pain and enables the grieving one to accept the loss and move on.

MILDRED TENGBOM
GRIEF FOR A SEASON

AS YOU THINK of things to ask your counselor, record them here immediately so they are not forgotten.

_____

_____

_____

_____

_____

_____

_____

_____

STATISTICS SHOW that grievers are especially vulnerable to illness and accidents when overly tired or under excessive stress. Here are some things you can do to help yourself and your counselor begin working through your intense grief, and on toward adjustment.

TAKE CARE OF YOURSELF—
- Get enough sleep.
- Eat well and slowly.
- Take vitamins, adding a "stress complex" tablet.
- Avoid excessive amounts of coffee and tea.
- Recognize that alcohol, cigarettes, tranquilizers and other drugs increase stress; they don't reduce it.
- Include regular exercise in your schedule.

RELAXATION TECHNIQUE — You can do much to manage your stress before it builds to the point of boiling over. Here is a simple exercise to do at your desk, on the bus, or while waiting for an appointment:

Step 1:   Close your eyes and get comfortable.
Step 2:   Take slow, deep breaths, exhaling completely.
Step 3:   With each breath, tell yourself to relax.
Step 4:   As you exhale, tell yourself that all your tension and stress are leaving with each breath.
Step 5:   Do this for several minutes until you feel your body begin to relax.
Step 6:   Repeat this exercise several times a day.

Handling the hardest days

ONE OF THE HARDER experiences for the griever is living through special days such as Christmas, Thanksgiving, anniversaries, and birthdays. These days once held the prospect of great joy, but now they are just another reminder of the loss you have suffered. Traditions seem meaningless without your lost one. What do you do?

There's no single best way for everyone to handle these difficult days; one approach works best for some, while another is better for others. That's why we've chosen to suggest a variety of ideas below.

But the bottom line for everyone is this: *Plan ahead for the bad days!* If you don't, you will be at the mercy of your emotions, which will ensure a difficult time for you and those around you.

FILL THEM FULL — One approach to handling the difficult days is to fill them full. Keep busy. Plan a full day of activities, and be with other people. By scheduling your day with as many activities as possible, you can keep yourself busy enough to not think too much about your loss.

KEEP THEM EMPTY — The opposite approach is to plan nothing so that you can cry, reflect, pray, or just be alone. Having a full day to cry is not all bad; but make sure you have someone to call in case you need to talk.

TIME FOR TRIBUTES — Another good idea is to have a specified time for everyone present to share a tribute to the deceased loved one, say at Christmas or Thanksgiving. By having a set time to reflect, proper tribute can be given and still allow everyone to enjoy the rest of the day without feeling guilty for having a good time.

VISIT THE MEMORIAL SITE — Plan a time during the special day to visit the memorial site or some other special place that the two of you enjoyed together. You may want to plan to take flowers, read a poem you have written, or write a letter to the deceased expressing how you feel.

START NEW TRADITIONS — Another approach to the special days is to begin new traditions. Intentionally set out to form new patterns. Do things you always wanted to do but didn't. Go see *The Nutcracker* or a Christmas program somewhere. Volunteer your time in a hospi-

*I affirm life;
I challenge problems;
I accept responsibility;
I believe God;
I live today!*

ELIZABETH SEARLE LAMB

tal, a food line for the needy, or a children's home. Take a meal to a needy family, and stay to enjoy it with them.

POST AN ALERT — If the special day coming up is an anniversary, birthday, or first-year anniversary of the death, alert people around you that it's coming. Tell your boss and co-workers, family and support group in advance so they will be prepared to give you the kind of support you'll need that day — such as phone calls, a redirection of your work load, playing cards with you, and so on. By planning ahead, others can help your day go more smoothly.

OTHER IDEAS —

- Take a trip with a friend on that special day.
- Go on a shopping spree, and buy yourself something new and dashing.
- Go to a funny movie…even a double feature.
- Do something physically active — tennis, bicycle riding, volleyball.
- Take a hot air balloon ride with a friend.

IN THE SPACES provided, make plans for the upcoming special days. Then take action to put your plans into motion.

our wedding anniversary _____

_____

_____

_____

_____

_____

first anniversary of loved one's death _____

_____

_____

_____

_____

_____

Planning ahead for special days

birthday _____

_____

_____

_____

_____

_____

_____

Thanksgiving _____

_____

_____

_____

_____

_____

Christmas _____

_____

_____

_____

_____

_____

_____

New Year's Eve and New Year's Day _____

_____

_____

_____

_____

_____

other holidays: _____

_____

_____

_____

_____

_____

You can live without someONE, if you have someTHING to live for.

206

ADJUSTMENT ALWAYS comes much slower than you want it to come. Just about the time you think you have "arrived," you feel yourself slip back into a phase of grief you thought you had already conquered. Hang in there! You *are* making progress.

Here are ways you can know healing has taken place.

1. You don't think about your lost one quite as much as you did at first.
2. You begin to make new plans for your own future.
3. You begin to feel better physically — and are able to take care of daily responsibilities.
4. You are not making as many irrational decisions as you did at first. And you're making more of your own decisions, rather than letting others make them for you.
5. You have returned to your normal eating and sleeping patterns.
6. You're not worrying so much about what might never happen.
7. You feel free to laugh again and have fun.
8. You're beginning to feel good about who you are and where you're going in life.

> ### Helping Others to Help
> Friends and family often care, but they do not know what to do. Most obviously they want to take away the pain, so when they cannot do that, they feel useless. If you "cope" quietly in times of pain, they feel shut out. Their love has no channel to express itself. It's like blocking a valve, causing a build-up of pressure behind. That causes them pain. Then your friends — the very ones who should be helping you — become the ones who need help in their pain. I believe that in the end it's you, the sufferer, who has to help them to help you. And that takes courage and understanding.
>
> JANE GRAYSHON
> IN TIMES OF PAIN

HOME SWEET HOME

14

Household Planning

Home Place

You say you went back there? How did it look? They've planted peach trees,
as we wanted to, outside the kitchen window? And screened the porch?…
Well, well, that's good…I only hope they never have to sell.
Go look at it myself? Well, no. Somehow I couldn't
say goodbye again — not now.

JANE MERCHANT
Because It's Here

IF YOU WERE LIVING with the deceased at the time of his or her death, one major area of your loss adjustment must take place at home. Your household has changed, and that means you must make some changes, too. This part of the adjustment to loss is often one of the most difficult because you are forced to deal with personal items that belonged to your lost one, as well as making difficult decisions about yourself. All that can be painful.

This section can help you with the many household decisions that must now be made.

Should I change my name listings?

SHOULD YOU LEAVE the name listing as it appears, or should you change it on various accounts? Only you can make that decision. Here are your primary options for each situation:

1. Leave the listing as it is.
2. Change to an unlisted service.
3. Change the name.

Considering these options, what do you think you should do about your utility accounts? (Option 2 — for unlisted service — will not always apply.)

telephone listing: _____

electric company: _____

gas company: _____

water department: _____

trash collection: _____

Should the name be changed on your bank/financial institution accounts?

bank/institution: *type of account:*   *option chosen:*

_____

_____

_____

_____

_____

_____

_____

_____

Should the name be changed on your charge accounts and/or credit cards?

account name: *account number:*   *option chosen:*

_____

_____

_____

_____

_____

_____

Should the name be changed on your subscription accounts?

publication title: *account number:*   *option chosen:*

_____

_____

_____

_____

_____

_____

_____

Should the name be changed on other personal accounts?

account name: *account number:*   *option chosen:*

_____

_____

_____

_____

_____

_____

_____

To move or stay?

IT'S FAIRLY SIMPLE to decide what name to put on various financial accounts, but other decisions are more complicated — such as whether to stay in the house you shared with your lost one, or move into a different residence. This decision involves several aspects of your life — social, emotional, and financial.

Sometimes what we *want* to do and what we are *able* to do are two different things. For instance, you may desire to stay in your current home, but you may no longer be able to afford it. So your emotional and financial life elements are at war, and you're caught in the middle.

Questions, questions, and more questions — at times they seem to almost drive you crazy. *Should I stay in my current home? Can I afford my present mortgage or rent payment? Can I afford the upkeep, the taxes, the insurance? Do I want to stay in my current surroundings, or do I need some new surroundings? Can I rent out my present home if I should move? Can I sell it?*

Perhaps the best way to visualize your decision is to do a comparison of your present residence and a new residence. In the following list, indicate with a check mark whether the advantage in each category lies more with the present address or a new address. If in some areas there is no particular advantage to either residence, leave the line blank.

When you've finished your comparison, count the number of check marks in each column and mark the totals on the "Total Advantages" line at the bottom. While the number of marks alone should not be the deciding factor (since some considerations are more important than others), it will help you see if there is a decided advantage of one over the other.

present residence:	consideration:	new residence:
_____	general location	_____
_____	mortgage/rent	_____
_____	utilities costs	_____
_____	amount of space	_____
_____	space to entertain others	_____
_____	privacy	_____
_____	security	_____
_____	place for automobile(s)	_____
_____	place for children to play	_____
_____	near grief support group	_____
_____	near personal counselor	_____
_____	near family	_____
_____	near friends	_____
_____	near employment	_____
_____	near church	_____
_____	near children's school(s)	_____
_____	near recreation areas	_____
_____	near mass transit	_____
_____	near post office	_____
_____	near bank	_____
_____	near doctor	_____
_____	near dentist	_____
_____	near accountant	_____
_____	near attorney	_____
_____	convenient to shopping	_____
_____	pets allowed	_____

_____	pets' freedom	_____
_____	lawn care	_____
_____	housekeeping cost	_____
_____	home maintenance	_____
_____	climate	_____
_____	personal allergies	_____
_____	children's allergies	_____
_____	city taxes	_____
_____	school taxes	_____
_____	state income taxes	_____
_____	near college/university	_____
_____	near arts/entertainment	_____
_____	volunteer opportunities	_____
_____	civic service opportunities	_____
_____	investment advantage	_____
_____	my personal preference	_____
_____	my children's preference	_____
_____	Total Advantages	_____

IF YOU DECIDE to change residences, the next consideration is about how to move. Take this quick inventory to see if you can avoid the high expense of hiring a professional moving company.

1. Do you have too many household goods to move yourself?
   yes___ no___
2. Are your household goods too heavy to move yourself?
   yes___ no___
3. Do you have friends or family who can help you move?
   yes___ no___
4. Do you have too many household goods for you and your friends or family to move easily? *yes___ no___*
5. Are your household goods too heavy for you and your friends or family to move? *yes___ no___*
6. Are you moving too far away for you and your friends or family to move you easily? *yes___ no___*
7. Are some of your household goods too valuable to risk moving yourself or with your friends' or family's help? *yes___ no___*

Moving expenses

8. Are there pieces of furniture that require special equipment to move (such as a piano)? _____

9. Can you pack everything you own yourself? *yes*___ *no*___

10. Can you and your friends or family pack everything you own? *yes*___ *no*___

11. Do you have enough protective coverings to keep your goods from being scratched or damaged during the move? *yes*___ *no*___

12. Can you cope emotionally with moving yourself right now? *yes*___ *no*___

Moving estimates

IF YOUR DECISION is to hire a professional moving company, the next step is to obtain at least two, preferably three, estimates from reputable firms. Ask your friends and family for recommendations about moving companies they have used successfully. Then call the firms and make arrangements for their representatives to come to your residence to provide you written estimates.

Moving estimates are typically based on the weight of your household goods, the distance involved in the move, how much packing the moving company will be asked to do versus how much you will do yourself, and general and special insurance costs.

company #1 — name: _____
contact person: _____
address: _____
city/state/zip: _____
telephone number: _____

company #2 — name: _____
contact person: _____
address: _____
city/state/zip: _____
telephone number: _____

company #3 — name: _____
contact person: _____
address: _____
city/state/zip: _____
telephone number: _____

ESTIMATE SUMMARY — To more easily compare the three estimates you have obtained, summarize them on the following chart.

description:	company 1:	company 2:	company 3:
estimated weight	_____	_____	_____
estimated mileage	_____	_____	_____
company packing cost	_____	_____	_____
general insurance cost	_____	_____	_____
special insurance cost	_____	_____	_____
loading date	_____	_____	_____
unloading date	_____	_____	_____
packing boxes cost	_____	_____	_____
wardrobe boxes cost	_____	_____	_____
other special costs	_____	_____	_____
	_____	_____	_____

Now, looking at the various considerations, which company has the best overall estimate for your move? _____
When you have made your decision, call that company to confirm the loading date, unloading date, the date when the packing boxes will be delivered, and other final arrangements.

IN THE SPACES PROVIDED below and on the next page, make a list of which categories of goods you will pack and which items you will ask the movers to pack. Refer to the written estimate provided by the chosen moving company to see which items are included in their estimate. Naturally, the more household goods you pack yourself, the less your final moving bill will be. But also be aware that the moving company may provide less insurance for the items you pack yourself. Anything requiring special handling and insurance should be packed by the company for maximum insurance recovery.

Your packing list

I'll pack these:	movers pack these:
_____	_____
_____	_____
_____	_____
_____	_____
_____	_____

I'll pack these: *movers pack these:*

_____   _____
_____   _____
_____   _____
_____   _____
_____   _____
_____   _____
_____   _____
_____   _____
_____   _____
_____   _____
_____   _____
_____   _____
_____   _____
_____   _____
_____   _____
_____   _____
_____   _____
_____   _____
_____   _____
_____   _____

Rental property checklist

SHOULD YOU DECIDE to rent or lease a new residence, this checklist will help you evaluate and compare various potential rental properties to see if they meet your standards, tastes and needs.

Suggestion: A great way to find an apartment to rent or lease without driving around town for hours and days is to use an apartment locator service, whose service is free to renters (Fees are paid by the apartment owner when you finally sign a lease.) These services are listed in the Yellow Pages. Just tell them what type of residence you're looking for — how big, the general location, preferred color schemes, the price you're willing to pay, whether you want a pool or not, your laundry needs, and the like. They'll find two or three places that meet your criteria and take you to look specifically at those. (The authors of this Guide have found this type of service to be fast, easy, and highly dependable.)

rental location #1:_____

house or apartment? _____

if apartment, name of complex: _____

landlord's name: _____

landlord's phone: _____

monthly rent: $ _____

payable where? _____when? _____

how long is that rate guaranteed? _____

late payment fee: $_____after _____day of the month

furnished or unfurnished? _____

appliances included: _____

_____

utilities paid by: you___ or landlord___?

if by you, estimated monthly utilities cost: $ _____

lawn maintenance by: you___ or landlord___?

if by landlord, is there an extra cost? _____

home repairs/maintenance by: you___ or landlord___?

if by landlord, what is extra cost? $ _____

deposit required: $ _____

deposit refund requirements: _____

approximate square footage: _____

garage? *yes___ no___* covered parking? *yes___ no___*

pool? *yes___ no___* tennis courts? *yes___ no___*

laundry room? *yes___ no___* where? _____

other facilities: _____

security system? *yes___ no___* if yes, describe: _____

_____

extra storage? *yes___ no___* party room? *yes___ no___*

party room deposit: $_____refund policy: _____

_____

pets allowed? *yes___ no___* deposit? *yes___ no___*

if yes, how much? $_____refund policy: _____

_____

hanging pictures allowed? *yes___ no___* restrictions: _____

_____

visitors permitted? *yes___ no___* restrictions: _____

_____

color scheme suitable? *yes___ no___* if no, will landlord repaint for you? *yes___ no___* can you? *yes___ no___*

rental location #2:_____

house or apartment? _____

if apartment, name of complex: _____

landlord's name: _____

landlord's phone: _____

monthly rent: $ _____

payable where? _____when? _____

how long is that rate guaranteed? _____

late payment fee: $_____after _____day of the month

furnished or unfurnished? _____

appliances included: _____

_____

utilities paid by: you___ or landlord___?

if by you, estimated monthly utilities cost: $ _____

lawn maintenance by: you___ or landlord___?

if by landlord, is there an extra cost? _____

home repairs/maintenance by: you___ or landlord___?

if by landlord, what is extra cost? $ _____

deposit required: $ _____

deposit refund requirements: _____

approximate square footage: _____

garage? *yes___ no___* covered parking? *yes___ no___*

pool? *yes___ no___* tennis courts? *yes___ no___*

laundry room? *yes___ no___* where? _____

other facilities: _____

security system? *yes___ no___* if yes, describe: _____

_____

extra storage? *yes___ no___* party room? *yes___ no___*

party room deposit: $_____refund policy: _____

_____

pets allowed? *yes___ no___* deposit? *yes___ no___*

if yes, how much? $_____refund policy: _____

_____

hanging pictures allowed? *yes___ no___* restrictions: _____

_____

visitors permitted? *yes___ no___* restrictions: _____

_____

color scheme suitable? *yes___ no___* if no, will landlord repaint for you? *yes___ no___* can you? *yes___ no___*

rental location #3:_____

house or apartment? _____

if apartment, name of complex: _____

landlord's name: _____

landlord's phone: _____

monthly rent: $ _____

payable where? _____when? _____

how long is that rate guaranteed? _____

late payment fee: $_____after _____day of the month

furnished or unfurnished? _____

appliances included: _____

_____

utilities paid by: you___ or landlord___?

if by you, estimated monthly utilities cost: $ _____

lawn maintenance by: you___ or landlord___?

if by landlord, is there an extra cost? _____

home repairs/maintenance by: you___ or landlord___?

if by landlord, what is extra cost? $ _____

deposit required: $ _____

deposit refund requirements: _____

approximate square footage: _____

garage? *yes___ no___* covered parking? *yes___ no___*

pool? *yes___ no___* tennis courts? *yes___ no___*

laundry room? *yes___ no___* where? _____

other facilities: _____

security system? *yes___ no___* if yes, describe: _____

_____

extra storage? *yes___ no___* party room? *yes___ no___*

party room deposit: $_____refund policy: _____

_____

pets allowed? *yes___ no___* deposit? *yes___ no___*

if yes, how much? $_____refund policy: _____

_____

hanging pictures allowed? *yes___ no___* restrictions: _____

_____

visitors permitted? *yes___ no___* restrictions: _____

_____

color scheme suitable? *yes___ no___* if no, will landlord repaint for
you? *yes___ no___* can you? *yes___ no___*

Selling your residence

IF YOU HAVE decided to sell your current residence, you can (1) sell the property yourself directly, or (2) sell the property through a licensed realtor. If you are a novice at selling a home, we recommend that you use a licensed realtor to help you.

It may also be worth your expense to have an attorney review the deed and the contract for the property you are selling.

Before showing your home to the realtor or potential buyers, make certain the house and property are as attractive as possible. Inside, an appealing atmosphere usually demands:

- good lighting
- airiness
- cleanness and neatness
- fragrant aromas
- necessary repairs completed
- fresh paint as needed
- proper room temperature

Don't forget the lawn either! Make sure the grass is neatly groomed, walks are swept, and so on. First impressions are lasting ones, and the realtor or buyer will see the outside of your home first. Make it a good first impression.

If you are using a realtor, it's usually best to be away from the house during a showing to potential buyers. If you are at home, remember to let the realtor sell *without your help.*

Buying a new residence

IF YOU'RE PURCHASING a new home, we again recommend the use of a licensed realtor or attorney to represent you.

Obtain as much information as possible concerning a property you may wish to buy. *Know* what you're getting for your money.

Don't forget the seller's real estate broker is responsible for disclosing any material information regarding the property. Getting as much initial information as possible from the seller — even if it becomes necessary to ask penetrating and possibly embarrassing questions — will pay off in the long run by saving both you and the agent from potential legal difficulties. The agent should also assume responsibility for searching the public records for such pertinent information as legal description, lot size, and yearly taxes. Use the following checklist to help you ask as many pertinent questions as possible about a property before you buy.

Remember also to consider important information about the neighborhood — including such factors as the nearness of friends and family, church, schools, and shopping.

address of property #1: _____

_____

listed price of property: _____

description of property in real estate listing: _____

_____

_____

name(s) and address of owner(s): _____

_____

accurate legal description of property: _____

_____

_____

size of lot (frontage and depth): _____

building square footage: _____ number of rooms: _____

construction and age of building: _____

_____

current annual property taxes: $ _____

amount of existing financing (including interest, payments, and

other costs):_____

average monthly utility payments: _____

appliances to be included in transaction: _____

_____

date property can be occupied/possessed: _____

possibility of seller financing? *yes*___ *no*___   (if yes, describe:)

_____

_____

zoning classification: _____

detailed list of what *will* and *will not* be included in the sales price:

_____

_____

_____

type of loan: _____

down payment: _____ monthly payments: _____

for how long? _____ interest rate: _____

major purchases required:

____ landscaping   ____ carpet   ____ window coverings

____ major appliances: _____

____ new roof   ____ foundation   ____ wiring

other: _____

address of property #2: _____

_____

listed price of property: _____

description of property in real estate listing: _____

_____

_____

_____

name(s) and address of owner(s): _____

_____

accurate legal description of property: _____

_____

_____

size of lot (frontage and depth): _____

building square footage: _____ number of rooms: _____

construction and age of building: _____

_____

current annual property taxes: $ _____

amount of existing financing (including interest, payments, and other costs):_____

average monthly utility payments: _____

appliances to be included in transaction: _____

_____

date property can be occupied/possessed: _____

possibility of seller financing? *yes*___ *no*___   (if yes, describe:)

_____

_____

zoning classification: _____

detailed list of what *will* and *will not* be included in the sales price:

_____

_____

_____

type of loan: _____

down payment: _____ monthly payments: _____

for how long? _____ interest rate: _____

major purchases required:

_____ landscaping   _____ carpet   _____ window coverings

_____ major appliances: _____

_____ new roof   _____ foundation   _____ wiring

other: _____

address of property #3: _____

_____

listed price of property: _____

description of property in real estate listing: _____

_____

_____

_____

name(s) and address of owner(s): _____

_____

accurate legal description of property: _____

_____

_____

size of lot (frontage and depth): _____

building square footage: _____ number of rooms: _____

construction and age of building: _____

_____

current annual property taxes: $ _____

amount of existing financing (including interest, payments, and
other costs):_____

average monthly utility payments: _____

appliances to be included in transaction: _____

_____

date property can be occupied/possessed: _____

possibility of seller financing? *yes___ no___*   (if yes, describe:)

_____

_____

zoning classification: _____

detailed list of what *will* and *will not* be included in the sales price:

_____

_____

_____

type of loan: _____

down payment: _____ monthly payments: _____

for how long? _____ interest rate: _____

major purchases required:

____ landscaping   ____ carpet   ____ window coverings

____ major appliances: _____

____ new roof   ____ foundation   ____ wiring

other: _____

Home furnishing plans

ITEMS TO KEEP: _____

_____

_____

_____

_____

_____

_____

_____

_____

_____

_____

_____

_____

_____

_____

_____

_____

ITEMS TO GIVE TO FAMILY MEMBERS AND FRIENDS:

item:	*recipient:*
_____	_____
_____	_____
_____	_____
_____	_____
_____	_____
_____	_____
_____	_____
_____	_____
_____	_____
_____	_____
_____	_____
_____	_____
_____	_____
_____	_____

_____   _____
_____   _____
_____   _____
_____   _____
_____   _____
_____   _____
_____   _____
_____   _____
_____   _____
_____   _____
_____   _____

ITEMS TO SELL OR DONATE TO CHARITY:

sell: *donate to charity:*

_____   _____
_____   _____
_____   _____
_____   _____
_____   _____
_____   _____
_____   _____
_____   _____
_____   _____
_____   _____
_____   _____
_____   _____
_____   _____
_____   _____
_____   _____
_____   _____
_____   _____
_____   _____
_____   _____
_____   _____

_____   _____
_____   _____
_____   _____
_____   _____
_____   _____
_____   _____
_____   _____
_____   _____
_____   _____
_____   _____
_____   _____
_____   _____

NEW ITEMS NEEDED:
  description: *cost:*

_____   _____
_____   _____
_____   _____
_____   _____
_____   _____
_____   _____
_____   _____
_____   _____
_____   _____
_____   _____
_____   _____
_____   _____
_____   _____
_____   _____
_____   _____
_____   _____
_____   _____
_____   _____
_____   _____

A PENNY SAVED

Financial Planning

> *Not what we give, but what we share,*
> *For the gift without the giver is bare;*
> *Who gives himself with his alms feeds three,*
> *Himself, his hungering neighbor and Me.*
>
> JAMES RUSSELL LOWELL

UNLESS YOU'RE A FINANCIAL WIZARD, facing the complex issues of arranging your finances for the future may worry or even frighten you. Unfortunately, most of us are not financial wizards, and dealing with money, securities, benefits, savings and investments is usually frustrating and intimidating. With the help of William G. "Bill" Southern, a highly qualified financial planner, we have developed this section to help you identify your present financial status and decide in which financial direction to move.

INFLATION, changing tax laws, fluctuating interest rates, and a variety of financial products have created a changeable and complicated financial environment. You can easily get lost in the maze of new financial information; yet, the following tasks must be accomplished nonetheless. You must...

- hedge yourself against inflation.
- reduce your income taxes.
- provide for yours or your children's education.
- increase your net worth.

Why and how to choose a financial planner

227

- plan for your retirement.
- use your insurance effectively.
- provide for a smooth disposition of your own estate someday.

You will need a variety of financial tools and procedures to create your own unique solutions to these complex problems. But a sound financial plan leads to a secure future.

If a qualified financial planner has not as yet been one of your professional advisers, we recommend choosing one. A financial planner can help you formulate your personal financial plan. And he can coordinate the efforts of all your other professional advisers (CPA, attorney, trust officer, and so on).

In choosing a financial planner, you should find a Charted Life Underwriter and Charted Financial Consultant (CLU and ChFC), a Certified Financial Planner (CFP), or an attorney who does financial and estate planning. You may contact your local organizations of the American Society of CLU/ChFC or the Estate Planning Council for help in locating someone.

Again, one of the best ways to find a suitable financial planner is to ask your professional and business friends for recommendations about qualified persons with whom they have had good experiences.

Budgeting: income vs. expenses

BUDGETING is the most important single phase of your financial plan. As you begin this new chapter in your life, budgeting may become even more important than before. Your success at budgeting will determine your peace of mind and financial security.

People fall into two financial planning categories. First, there are those who *spend first* and then save if there is any money left. Second, there are those who *save first* and then spend or live on what is left of their pay check.

Surprisingly, about 96 percent of people are included in the first group — the spenders — while the savers make up only 4 percent. But here's an important point to remember: Spenders always end up working for savers! In which group do you want to be? Fortunately, the choice is yours to make.

A SIMPLE FORMULA for budgeting that has worked well for both wealthy and medium-income people has only four parts. Fill in the blanks indicated with your personal financial information for a better picture of how your healthy financial percentages should look.

YOUR GROSS INCOME $_____ = **100%**
(Before taxes or deductions)

First, pay yourself. $_____ = **10%**
(This should go in savings, but not
with a "put-it-in, take-it-out" attitude)

Second, give it away. $_____ = **10%**
(Give to your church or other charitable
organization. The Law of Nature says,
"Whatever you give away without ex-
pecting any return, comes back to you
multiplied.")

Third, use for income replacement. $_____ = **10%**
(You should allot this amount to replace
your income in the event of loss of
income due to (1) living too long —
retirement, (2) not living long enough —
yet your dependents' needs continue; and
(3) illness or injury that leaves you unable
to work — disability income protection.)

Fourth, pay taxes and spend. $_____ = **70%**
(Pay FICA and income taxes, then live
on the rest, but account for where
you spend it. If you are able to
live on less than 70%, increase
each of the first three percentages
proportionately.)

NOTE: People who live by this formula rarely have any financial problems.

When your outgo exceeds your income, then your upkeep is your downfall.

Your monthly budget

YOU MAY FIND IT USEFUL to compare your own saving and spending habits with our national averages. (For this comparison "medium income" assumes a budget with monthly expenditures of $2,500 for a family of four; "high income" assumes monthly expenditures of $6,000 for a family of four; averages for donations to church and charities not included.)

	FAMILY WITH MEDIUM INCOME		FAMILY WITH HIGH INCOME	
	monthly outlay	percent of budget	monthly outlay	percent of budget
savings & investments	0	0.0	$415	6.97
medical care & insurance	$102	4.0	260	4.3
food and dining	530	20.9%	750	12.5%
shelter & household expenses	582	23.0	1,320	22.0
transportation	201	8.0	460	7.6
clothing & personal care	201	8.0	380	6.3
federal income tax	530	21.0	1,640	27.33
other taxes & Social Security	241	9.5	400	6.66
other consumption	140	5.6	375	6.2
TOTAL	$2,527	100.0%	$6,000	100.0%

(SOURCE: TOUCHE ROSS & COMPANY)

In the spaces below, enter current spending figures for your own family, then calculate the percentages for each line by dividing your total monthly outlay into the figure for each area.

	monthly outlay	percent of budget
savings & investments	$ _____	_____
church & charities	_____	_____
medical care & insurance	_____	_____
food & dining	_____	_____
shelter & household expenses	_____	_____
transportation	_____	_____
clothing & personal care	_____	_____
federal income tax	_____	_____
other taxes & Social Security	_____	_____
other consumption	_____	_____
TOTAL	$ _____	100%

CHECK YOURSELF — Perform a quick check on yourself now. Answer the following questions honestly and thoughtfully.

1. Do my percentages fall close to the "Formula for Financial Success?" *yes___ no___*
2. Are my percentages close to the national averages? *yes___ no___*
3. Do I want to make any adjustments to my spending habits to move my percentages closer to the savers? *yes___ no___*
4. What adjustments am I willing to make?

_____

_____

If your answer to question 3 is yes, discuss your decision with your financial adviser. Ask for suggestions of ways to rearrange your spending to begin moving gradually toward a more healthy financial profile.

YOUR NEW BUDGET — Ask your financial planner to help you plan a new budget as outlined in the spaces provided below. Then figure the new projected budget percentages by dividing the total monthly expenditure figure into each of the budget item figures.

Caution: Don't expect to be able to change your spending patterns all at once to reach your ultimate percentage goals. These financial adjustments take time and patience. If your financial picture is not entirely rosy, it likely did not get into that condition overnight. Neither will you be able to correct it overnight. Take small steps to reach your goal, but take them.

	monthly outlay	percent of budget
savings & investments	$ _____	_____
church & charities	_____	_____
medical care & insurance	_____	_____
food & dining	_____	_____
shelter & household expenses	_____	_____
transportation	_____	_____
clothing & personal care	_____	_____
federal income tax	_____	_____
other taxes & Social Security	_____	_____
other consumption	_____	_____
TOTAL	$ _____	100%

How to improve your cash flow

TO *INCREASE* CASH INFLOW —

1. Work harder (or smarter). Investing in yourself to improve your earning potential may prove to be your best investment.
2. Make your assets work harder by improving your income yields or achieving capital growth.

TO *DECREASE* CASH OUTFLOW:

1. Reduce your income taxes.
2. Manage your available cash better by budgeting.
3. Protect yourself from unforeseen losses (such as death, disability, liability, or property loss).

Remember, most people spend first and try to save or invest what little is left. Few people set aside a definite amount first and spend the balance. People who spend first usually end up with little or no savings or investments.

It's also true that people who *save first* accumulate dollars for education of their children, retirement, and other worthwhile objectives. In other words, people who save first generally have money when they really need it.

Fortunately, you have the power to choose what you will do.

Planning for your financial future

JUST AS DEVELOPING a realistic budget is important as you begin your new life, planning for your financial security is even more important. Money and financial security play a vital role in the healthy adjustment to loss.

You should take a "financial physical," just as you would take a medical physical. Your financial planner can help you develop a short-term and long-term financial plan. He will help you think about what type of financial goals you want to achieve and by what time you want these goals to be accomplished.

Along with a list of your goals, the following documents will be needed for an analysis by your financial planner in order for him to prepare a personal financial plan for you. Put a check mark by each item below as you have collected it for review by your financial planner.

__ your most recent payroll stub.
__ your most recent federal income tax return.
__ your personal employment benefit statements.
__ your company benefit plan booklets (group benefits, pension, etc.)
__ your will.
__ any trust arrangements in which you may be involved.

any business arrangements in which you are involved:
__ buy/sell
__ deferred compensation
__ stock option/bonus plans

your insurance and/or annuity contracts:
__ life insurance policies
__ hospital and major medical insurance
__ disability insurance
__ automobile insurance
__ property and casualty

__ evidence of any inheritance you will receive from the deceased.
__ evidence of any other inheritances you will receive.
__ copies of mortgages, loans, and contracts in effect.
__ last statements from your creditors and investments (such as MasterCard, VISA, stocks, bonds, mutual funds, etc.)

PERSONALLY YOURS

16

Planning My Future

LIVING ALONE is the most difficult adjustment many loss survivors face. Constant quietness, involuntary self-sufficiency, lack of physical touching, and the necessity of making decisions without the benefit of feedback — all these require adjustments that seem impossible.

However, not everyone looks at living alone the same way. Some will even consider the experience a relief. Living alone is not always easy, but it's not a curse either. After all, being independent and self-sufficient leads to many opportunities. The one ingredient that will determine the outcome is your *attitude* about living alone. You can ensure failure by your negative attitude, or you can enhance your chance for success by having a positive attitude. The choice is yours.

Since attitude is so important, notice the following list of key attitudes and consider their validity. Indicate with a check mark whether you agree or disagree with these statements.

Learning to live alone

Agree	Disagree	
_____	_____	1. Aloneness and loneliness are not the same.

1. Aloneness and loneliness are not the same.
   - Some of the loneliest people in the world are married.
   - Everyone feels lonely at times, whether in or out of relationships.
   - Loneliness is feeling alone, even in the midst of a crowd (disconnected).
   - Aloneness is being alone, yet still in love (connected).

2. Even though you feel lonely, you are a person with the ability to make your own decisions.
   - Some married folks would cherish your independence.
   - As a single adult, you can do what you want when you want.
   - You may experience guilt feelings when you begin to make your own decisions, especially when you are used to participating in joint decisions.

3. Your time is your own.
   - Spur-of-the-moment decisions will affect others less now than before.
   - You can do something just for you. Pamper yourself. Read the book you always wanted to.

4. You can decide to do what you want to do around the house or apartment, such as:
   - Change wallpaper, paint, put in new carpet.
   - Dress any way you like.
   - Watch the TV programs you want to see.

5. Eating is now your freedom of choice. You can choose:
   - How much.
   - When and how often.
   - What kind.

Agree   Disagree

_____ _____ 6. You can decide to spend money any way you want. *Your only limitation is your budget.*

_____ _____ 7. Cleaning is another area of freedom.
- When you do clean house, it's for yourself.
- If it's dirty, there's no one to blame but you.
- A clean house probably will make you feel better.

_____ _____ 8. You can entertain exactly as you like.
- Invite whomever you wish.
- Schedule visits to fit your convenience.
- Just because you're single doesn't mean you don't have friends. Invite them over! Don't be alone if you don't want to be.

_____ _____ 9. Living alone provides opportunities for renewal, in terms of:
- Physical health (nutrition, exercise, rest).
- Mental health (emotional healing).
- Education (classes, professional training).
- Hobbies (learning new ones, renewing old ones).

_____ _____ 10. Vocational freedom often returns when living alone.
- You can work longer hours if you like.
- You become free to travel.
- You can commit undivided energy and attention to your work.

My first act of freedom will be to believe in freedom.

WILLIAM JAMES

If any or all of these items are true for you, they are true because you have chosen to make them true. Our outlook on life is a choice. However, in most cases, the griever would gladly give up any or all of those freedoms if his or her loved one could be returned to life. Since that cannot happen, making the most of your new life is the best way to go.

Free to be me

LIST HERE any other personal freedoms you can think of that are unique to your own situation, and describe how you will now exercise that freedom to be yourself.

_____
_____
_____
_____
_____
_____
_____
_____
_____
_____
_____
_____
_____
_____
_____
_____
_____
_____
_____
_____

A man alone, a woman alone

DO MEN OR WOMEN find it harder to live alone? —
The answer is both, but for different reasons. Those reasons are dependent on the roles that each survivor must now fill in the absence of the lost one. Typically, men have a more difficult time adjusting to domestic roles. Women's difficulties, however, stem from identity adjustments and fears. Read through the following list and check yourself to see which difficulties you are experiencing due to your loss.

Women's difficulties—
- _Uncertain identity._ Women over forty were not brought up in a career-oriented society. Being a mother, wife, mate, and household manager is where identity has been built. When these roles are taken away, self-identity is often questioned.

- *Financial insecurity.* Studies show that within five years following the death of a male spouse, family income is reduced by an average of forty-four percent.
- *Fears.* Women who have lost their mate measure significantly higher on fear issues than do men who have lost their wives. In addition to financial insecurity, widows fear crime, living alone, and being taken advantage of in the marketplace.
- *Household upkeep.* The gender problem is most acute in the area of mechanical, electrical, plumbing, and roofing skills. This is especially true when a woman has little or no working knowledge in such areas.
- *Dating.* Dating is an area of particular difficulty for a variety of reasons. First, women past age fifty outnumber men by a ratio of five to one. In addition to the disproportionate number of women in this age bracket, women complain that the rules of dating have changed. They no longer know what acceptable dating behavior is. Who pays? Who drives? Who calls whom? What is considered appropriate dress? Finding one's comfort zones in these areas takes time and often painful experience.

Men's difficulties—
- *Domestic situations.* Men often don't seem to function well in organizing the household, shopping, cooking, and cleaning — roles traditionally filled at home by women.
- *Relational support.* The achievement-oriented male may be doing well professionally but at the same time be hurting in the relational arena. If one's ego is built on professional accomplishments, it's safe to assume he has not invested large amounts of time or energy in building and maintaining a support network.
- *Communicating vulnerability.* Knowing and verbalizing your feelings are important in the grieving process. But this is hard to learn for a male who has suppressed his feelings all his life, and living alone with no one to talk with further complicates the problem.

New relationships

GIVE YOURSELF this short Relationship Assessment Survey. Answer the questions candidly and honestly. This will help you have a picture of how you see yourself in relationship to others. Finish each statement as completely as you can.

The scary thing about new relationships is...

_____
_____
_____
_____
_____
_____

When I feel lonely...

_____
_____
_____
_____
_____
_____

The things I miss most in an intimate relationship are...

1. _____   6. _____
   _____   _____
2. _____   7. _____
   _____   _____
3. _____   8. _____
   _____   _____
4. _____   9. _____
   _____   _____
5. _____   10. _____
   _____   _____

The things I like most about not being attached are…

1. _____
2. _____
3. _____
4. _____
5. _____

6. _____
7. _____
8. _____
9. _____
10. _____

The assets I have to share in a relationship are…

1. _____
2. _____
3. _____
4. _____
5. _____

6. _____
7. _____
8. _____
9. _____
10. _____

Before adjustment to a loss is completed, tension will arise stemming from the longing to love and be loved without being in a healthy position to act on that longing. Relationships with meaning, depth, and commitment don't just happen; they are created slowly and intentionally, like masterpieces of art. Unfortunately, the times that meaningful relationships are needed the most are the very times grievers are least prepared to build healthy new ones.

Relationships that are healthy require energy, emotional health, and mental stability. Under the best of circumstances, building a mutually healthy relationship is a difficult task. A griever inevitably brings his or her grief into a new relationship and doubles the responsibilities. You cannot invest the energy and emotions required for healthy grieving while at the same time investing the time, energy, and emotions needed to create a healthy new relationship. What's needed most is time to complete one process (grieving) before starting the second (building a new intimate relationship).

For that reason, the standard time frame suggested for grievers to remain in an uncommitted single state is two years. This allows time to complete the grief process without complicating a new relationship. The time frame may differ from one person to the next. For example, if the loss through death came suddenly or unnaturally, adjustment time generally is longer.

Masterpiece

You don't slap a masterpiece together with a bucket of paint and a roller. It's painted slowly, one gentle stroke at a time, with a fine-line brush and loving hands. You pay attention to minute details, hues of color, and duplicating the art of the Great Artist. Anyone can paint an ordinary wall, but a masterpiece is obviously the work of a caring artist who wants to create a classic — something beautiful that will last through the ages.

MARY HOLLINGSWORTH

Dating again

SOME SINGLE men and women decide they are not interested in marrying again, and busy themselves with children, grandchildren, friends, hobbies, and activities. Many more are anxious to find a special someone with whom to settle down again. The questions are "How?" and "Where do I start?"

START AT HOME — If you want to begin dating, start by telling your friends, family, and acquaintances. People close to you may not offer to introduce you to other available singles for fear of offending or upsetting you, or for fear of seeming disloyal to the memory of your lost one. So begin by sharing your desires discreetly with those closest to you, and let them begin thinking of people who might be right for you.

GO WHERE AVAILABLE PEOPLE CONGREGATE — Having others look for you is great, but you must be willing to look for yourself, too. For instance, you may want to join any of a number of organizations where available people with interests similar to yours can be found. You never know who will be there, and doing things in groups at first is safe and fun. Perhaps you can begin by finding out the names, numbers, and meeting times of potential interest groups.

CHURCH: _____

address: _____

_____

phone: _____

specific group name: _____

meeting time: _____

meeting place: _____

_____

SERVICE CLUB: _____

address: _____

_____

phone: _____

meeting time: _____

meeting place: _____

membership requirements: _____

_____

_____

HOBBY CLUB: _____

address: _____

_____

phone: _____

specific hobby: _____

meeting time: _____

meeting place: _____

membership requirements: _____
_____
_____
_____

POLITICAL GROUP: _____
address: _____
_____
phone: _____
purpose: _____
meeting time: _____
meeting place: _____
membership requirements: _____
_____
_____

SPORTS CLUB: _____
address: _____
_____
phone: _____
specific sports: _____
_____
meeting time: _____
meeting place: _____
membership requirements: _____
_____
_____

TRAVEL CLUB: _____
address: _____
_____
phone: _____
purpose: _____
meeting time: _____
meeting place: _____
membership requirements: _____
_____
_____

FINE ARTS GROUP: _____
address: _____
_____
phone: _____
specific emphasis: _____
_____
meeting time: _____
meeting place: _____
membership requirements: _____
_____
_____

WORKSHOP: _____
where held: _____
address: _____
_____
phone: _____
workshop description: _____
_____
teacher's name: _____
dates: _____
time: _____
enrollment requirements: _____
_____
_____

EDUCATIONAL CLASS: _____
where taught: _____
address: _____
_____
phone: _____
class content: _____
_____
teacher's name: _____
dates of class: _____
times: _____
enrollment requirements: _____
_____
_____

VOLUNTEER ORGANIZATION: _____

location for volunteer work: _____

_____

address: _____

_____

phone: _____

volunteer times: _____

training required: _____

_____

other requirements: _____

_____

_____

_____

HAVE AVAILABLE PEOPLE OVER — Going where people are is good, but your greatest joy may be in entertaining. So take the initiative to invite others over. Having guests into your home can be fun in a safe environment, especially when the gathering is of people you know and feel comfortable with. You may even try inviting single friends, telling them to bring a friend of the opposite sex who they are not personally interested in. It's a great way to meet new people.

You might want to start with a relatively small group. Think of several people you can invite, then write their names and phone numbers below. When you are ready, you can then call them up quickly and invite them to come, asking them to bring a friend of the opposite sex.

name: _____	name: _____
phone: _____	phone: _____
name: _____	name: _____
phone: _____	phone: _____
name: _____	name: _____
phone: _____	phone: _____
name: _____	name: _____
phone: _____	phone: _____
name: _____	name: _____
phone: _____	phone: _____

name: _____	name: _____
phone: _____	phone: _____
name: _____	name: _____
phone: _____	phone: _____
name: _____	name: _____
phone: _____	phone: _____
name: _____	name: _____
phone: _____	phone: _____
name: _____	name: _____
phone: _____	phone: _____
name: _____	name: _____
phone: _____	phone: _____
name: _____	name: _____
phone: _____	phone: _____
name: _____	name: _____
phone: _____	phone: _____
name: _____	name: _____
phone: _____	phone: _____

Ice-breakers for small groups

PERHAPS IT'S BEEN A WHILE since you've done any entertaining, especially of single people. We thought you might need a few suggestions about how to get successful parties off to a good start. These ideas come from singles of all ages who are members of a 600-member singles group at a church in the Dallas-Fort Worth metroplex. They enjoyed them; your group probably will too.

A HAT PARTY — Gather up as many different hats — any kind of hats — as you have people coming to your party. Purchase a couple of small door prizes. Before the guests arrive, put a small sticker inside the crown of one or two hats. Also, put on one of the hats yourself before you answer the door the first time. As guests arrive, ask each one to don a hat with you for the evening. They can choose any one of the hats available. During the party, periodically say, "Okay, let's swap hats." Have everyone trade hats with someone else. Repeat the hat-swat routine about three or four times during the evening. Later, ask them to look in the crown of their hats to see who has a small sticker there, and announce that this person (or those persons) will win a small door prize. At the end of the evening, take a group hat picture. The next day get the film developed and have enough copies of the photo made to give one to each person who attended the party. They'll love it!

GETTING-TO-KNOW-YOU PARTY — After everyone has arrived for the party, distribute big pieces of manila or photocopy paper (at least eleven by seventeen inches), plus colored marking pens to each person. Have each person put his or her name at the top of the paper. Then ask each one to put "Things I Like" on one side of the paper and "Things I Dislike" on the other side. Then ask them to list three or four things about themselves under each category. (such as "travel!" or "Italian food" or "tennis" under "Things I Like," and "spinach" or "opera" under "Things I Dislike." Put all the papers on a table somewhere, along with the marking pens. During the evening ask everyone to look at the papers and add their own comments and first names to other people's papers. For instance, if you love Italian food, you might write on that person's paper, "Me, too! Let's go to lunch at Mama Leone's next week. Margaret." At the end of the evening, each person takes his own paper home to remind him of those with whom he shares interests in common. It's a fun way to find other people who share one another's interests and, perhaps, to get some new friendships started.

POLAROID SCAVENGER HUNT — Divide your party group into smaller groups of, say, four each. Give each group a Polaroid camera with film. Also give them a list of items to be photographed. Then send them off on a scavenger hunt. The first group back with photos of all the items on their list wins. The key is making the list of items fun and challenging. Items might include such things as "a waiter singing 'Hello Dolly,'" "the street sign at Broadway and Fifth," "a bus driver by his bus," and so on..

This works equally well as an "audio scavenger hunt," where you use portable tape recorders and a list of sounds, rather than the Polaroid.

HERE ARE SIMPLE, but practical, rules to consider when you decide to get back into the dating arena.

1. Accept the fact that the world may have changed since you last dated. For instance, on occasion women now call men for dates, and sometimes they even pay.
2. Don't allow yourself to be pressured, badgered or shamed into acting contrary to your own standards and beliefs. Just because others do certain things doesn't mean you must. There are men and women who will respect and appreciate your beliefs.
3. Let others know where you are going and with whom. Don't be too naive. Safety is the rule.
4. Don't build your entire life around searching for a new mate. Get interested in other things, too. Remember: Interested people are interesting; bored people are boring.
5. Go out and have some fun! Be creative in thinking of things to do together. You need to see a new person in all types of settings in order to fully get to know him or her.
6. Don't assume that all dates have to cost lots of money to be fun. In fact, many times it's the inexpensive dates that are the best. Consider doing some of the inexpensive things on the following list from time to time, rather than "painting the town red."

Go on a picnic.
Take a two-hour hike or back-packing trip.
Go bicycle riding.
Go window shopping.
Play tennis or some other two-player sport.
Play indoor board games.
Read a book together.
Rent movies, make popcorn, and stay in.
Wash your cars together.
Plant a garden together.
Make and fly a kite together.
Bake cookies together for someone else.
Go to church together.
Go to the library together.
Go to a county or state fair.
Go to garage or estate sales.
Do volunteer work together.

Work a jigsaw puzzle.
Go to a museum.
Collect something together.
Do a hobby together.
Make a sand castle on the beach.
Make a snowman.
Jog together.
Make homemade ice cream and invite some friends over.

Will I remarry?

BEFORE YOU DECIDE whether or not to remarry, it's important for you to do a personal assessment to determine your reasons for remarrying or not. Consider these things:

Healthy relationships are built on a balance of need.

- *I have a need for someone to fill my void.* As relational beings, when an intimate relationship is altered by death, it is natural to miss the experience of intimacy. Many people see a new relationship — someone with whom to spend time, and share burdens, joys, and experiences — as the only viable cure for loneliness.

  The things I need in a new relationship are...

  _____
  _____
  _____
  _____

- *I have a need to give to someone else.* The need to receive from someone else is not enough to make a healthy relationship work because someone else can never make you happy. Happiness must reside within you so that it can be shared, not made. The same is true of joy, love, and peace. When a person possesses these emotions, they must be shared to be complete. Thus, the need to give opens the door to vulnerability and intimacy.

  The things I need to share in a relationship are...

  _____
  _____
  _____
  _____

Healthy relationships are built around likes.

- *Personality attractions.* Some personalities seem to blend naturally. It's pleasant being with a certain person simply because the two of you like being together. Friendship grows because it seems as if it were meant to be.
  The personality traits I like most in others are...

  _____

  _____

  _____

  _____

- *Activity preferences.* Is it true that having someone with whom to share the joy of an experience increases the pleasure of that experience? It is true only if the person you're with enjoys the same thing you do. If having someone to share life's experiences is important, then having common interests with that person is important to the health of that relationship.
  The activities that bring me the greatest joy are...

  _____

  _____

  _____

  _____

- *Attractions.* Being physically attracted to another person is something most people relate to, but few really understand. Either the attraction is present in a relationship or it's not. However, liking and loving are not the same thing, and they are often confused. You may love someone out of attraction or infatuation, yet you may still not *like* him. Make sure your love is first based on like, not the other way around.
  Love is ... _____

  _____

  _____

  Like is... _____

  _____

  _____

Healthy relationships are built on character.

- *Admiring another's moral character.* Having similar likes and dislikes in activities is important to the dynamics of a relationship. In the same way, sharing similar values, ethics, and moral standards is also important. Admiration grows when those values are demonstrated and shared.

The moral values I will never compromise are...

_____

_____

_____

- *Ability to commit.* Without commitment, a secure relationship is never possible. Trust, trustworthiness, and confidence are all made possible when the ability to commit is present in a person. The best way to tell whether a person has this ability is by the integrity of his past. One's history speaks louder than words or even good intentions. As the old saying goes, "It's tough for a tiger to change his stripes."

  The hardest thing about trusting another person is...

  _____

  _____

  _____

Summary

HEALTHY RELATIONSHIPS are built by two healthy people who bring their health to the relationship and share their health with each other. In this way they create a healthy relationship pattern capable of addressing, in a healthy manner, the sick and wounded areas of each of the two persons.

REMEMBER: **A relationship cannot be healthier than the two persons who form it.**

YOUR LOSS ADJUSTMENT LIBRARY

IN RECENT MONTHS AND YEARS excellent books, tapes, and videos have been written and produced to help us with grief, death, and dying. You may find one or more of these resources to be of help to you during some phase of your grief process.

A caution: Some of these books, while containing helpful insights, may suggest an unrealistic time frame for grieving, or may stereotype grievers unfairly. Remember, there is no set timetable for grief, and each person's grief process is unique. Take your time, and do it your way.

Many of these books may be available at your public library. Some can also be found in your local bookstore; if your bookstore does not carry a title you want to purchase, ask if the store will order it for you from the publisher.

In addition to the books listed here, consider also to the video presentation *Grief Recovery* by Chaplain Larry Yeagley, Adventist Life Seminars, Route 1, Box 248, Crystal Springs, MS 39059. (601) 892-5559.

Grief

Death: The Final Stage of Growth by Elizabeth Kubler-Ross, Prentice Hall, Box 500, Englewood Cliffs, NJ 07632.

Don't Take My Grief Away from Me by Doug Manning, In-sight Books, P.O. Box 1784, Ann Arbor, MI 48106.

Good Grief by Granger E. Westburg, Fortress Press, 2900 Queen Lane, Philadelphia, PA 19129.

Hope for Bereaved (Understanding, Coping and Growing Through Grief) by Hope for Bereaved, 1342 Lancaster Avenue, Syracuse, NY 13210.

Living through Personal Crisis by Ann K. Stearns, Thomas Moore Press, 223 W. Erie Street, Chicago, IL 60611.

Living When a Loved One Has Died by Earl Grollman, Beacon Press, PO Box 527, Kansas City, MO 64141.

On Death and Dying by Elizabeth Kubler-Ross, Macmillan Company, 866 Third Avenue, New York, NY 10022.

The Many Faces of Grief by Edgar N. Jackson, Abingdon Press, 201 Eighth Avenue, S., Nashville, TN 37202.

Every person who knows how to read has it in his power to magnify himself, to multiply the ways in which he exists, to make his life full, significant and interesting.

ALDOUS HUXLEY

What Helped Me When My Loved One Died, edited by Earl Grollman, Beacon Press, Beacon Press, PO Box 527, Kansas City, MO 64141.

When Bad Things Happen to Good People by Rabbi Kushner, Avon Books, 1790 Broadway, New York, NY 10019.

When Going to Pieces Holds You Together by William Miller, Augsburg Publishing House, 426 S. Fifth Street, Minneapolis, MN 55415.

When Someone Dies by Edgar N. Jackson, Fortress Press, 2900 Queen Lane, Philadelphia, PA 19129.

When Your Friend Is Grieving by Paula D'Arcy, Harold Shaw Publishers, Box 567, Wheaton, IL 60187.

Where Is God When It Hurts? by Philip Yancey, Zondervan, 1420 Robinson Road, S.E., Grand Rapids, MI 49506.

Bereaved Parents

After Suicide by John A. Hewett, The Westminster Press, 512 E. Main Street, Richmond, VA 23219.

The Bereaved Parent by Harriett S. Schiff, Penquin Books, Inc., 40 W. 23rd Street, New York, NY 10010.

Recovering from the Loss of a Child by Katherine F. Donnelly, Macmillan Company, 866 Third Avenue, New York, NY 10022.

Suicide: Prevention, Intervention, Postvention by Earl Grollman, Beacon Press, PO Box 527, Kansas City, MO 64141.

When Pregnancy Fails: Families Coping with Miscarriage, Stillbirth and Newborn Death by Lasker & Borg, Beacon Press, PO Box 527, Kansas City, MO 64141.

Widowed

Alone by Katie Wiebe, Tyndale House, 336 Gundersen Drive, Wheaton, IL 60187.

Survival Handbook for Widows (and for Relatives and Friends Who Want to Understand) by Ruth Jean Loweinsohn, American Association of Retired Persons (AARP), 3200 E. Carson Street, Lakewood, CA 90712.

When Your Spouse Dies by Cathleen L. Curry, Ave Maria Press, Notre Dame, IN 46556.

Parent's Death

Learning to Say Goodbye When a Parent Dies by Eda Le Shan, Macmillan Company, 866 Third Avenue, New York, NY 10022.

How It Feels When a Parent Dies by Jill Krementz, Alfred A. Knopf, Inc., Random House Publishers, 201 E. 50th Street, New York, NY 10022.

Books for Children

Anne and the Sand Dobbies (A Story about Death for Children & Parents) by John Coburn, Seabury Press, 815 Second Avenue, New York, NY 10017.

About David by Susan B. Pfeffer, Dell Publishing, 1 Dag Hammarskjold Plaza, 245 E. 47th Street, New York, NY 10017.

Death Be Not Proud by John Gunther, Harper & Row Publishers, Inc., Icehouse One-401, 151 Union Street, San Francisco, CA 94111-1299.

Hope for the Flowers by Trina Paulus, Paulist Press, 545 Island Road, Ramsey, NJ 07446.

The Butterfly Tree by Joan L. Nixon, Our Sunday Visitor, Inc., 200 Noll Plaza, Huntington, IN 46750.

The Fall of Freddie the Leaf (A Story of Life For All Ages) by Leo Buscaglia, Holt, Reinhart & Winston, Inc., 383 Madison Avenue, New York, NY 10017.

The Velveteen Rabbit by Margery Williams, Avon Books, 1790 Broadway, New York, NY 10019.

Tunnel Vision by Fran Arrick, Dell Publishing, 1 Dag Hammarskjold Plaza, 245 E. 47th Street, New York, NY 10017.

When My Dad Died by Janice M. Hammond, Cranbrook Publishing, 2815 Cranbrook, Ann Arbor, MI 48104.

When My Mommy Died by Janice M. Hammond, Cranbrook Publishing, 815 Cranbrook, Ann Arbor, MI 48104.

Why Did Grandpa Die? by Barbara S. Hazen, a Little Golden Book.

Murder

Murder: This Could Never Happen to Me (A Handbook for Families of Murder Victims and People Who Assist Them), A Project of the Mental Health Association of Tarrant County, 3136 W. Fourth Street, Fort Worth, TX 76107. (817) 335-5405.

No Time for Goodbye by Janice H. Lord, Pathfinder Publishing, Ventura, CA.

The Crime Victim's Book by Bard & Sangrey, Citadel Press, Secaucus, NJ.

What Murder Leaves Behind (The Victim's Family) by Doub Magee, Dodd, Mead & Company, 79 Madison Avenue, New York, NY 10016.

Gift Books for Grievers

It's A One-derful Life! — A Single's Celebration by Mary Hollingsworth, Brownlow Publishing, 6309 Airport Freeway, Fort Worth, TX 76117.

To Heal Again (Towards Serenity and the Resolution of Grief) by Rusty Berkus, Red Rose Press, PO Box 24, Eucino, CA 91426.

The Everyday Bible, New Century Version, Word, Inc., 5221 N. O'Connor Road, Irving, TX 75039.

The Complete Poems of Emily Dickinson by Emily Dickinson, Little, Brown & Company, 34 Beacon Street, Boston, MA 02106.

The Prophet by Kahil Gibran, Alfred A. Knopf, Random House Publishers, 210 E. 50th Street, New York, NY 10022.

Rainbows: A Book of Trust through Troubled Times by Mary Hollingsworth, The C. R. Gibson Company, Knight Street, Norwalk, CT 06856-9974.

These, then, are my last words

to you:

Be not afraid of life.

Believe that life is worth living,

and your belief will help

create the fact.

WILLIAM JAMES
THE WILL TO BELIEVE